DEVI — *The Mother-Goddess*
An Introduction

To the gods
and to the demons
who dance in my dreams

Mahadevi, the embodiment of the
universe; South Indian bronze

DEVI
The Mother-Goddess

An Introduction

Devdutt Pattanaik

Vakils, Feffer and Simons Pvt. Ltd.
Hague Building, 9, Sprott Road, Ballard Estate,
Mumbai 400 001

First printing 2000
Second printing 2002
Third printing 2005

Price in India Rs. 295/-

Published by Bimal Mehta
for Vakils, Feffer and Simons Pvt. Ltd.
Hague Building, 9, Sprott Road, Ballard Estate
Mumbai 400 001. India

Printed by Arun K. Mehta at Vakil & Sons Pvt. Ltd.
Industry Manor, Appasaheb Marathe Marg
Worli, Mumbai 400 025. India

ISBN 81-87111-45-3

Contents

Acknowledgements

My parents, who have always been there for me

Dr. Usha Bhatia, Guruji Brothers, Giri, Shailaja, Arun K. and Mr. R. G. Singh of Handicrafts Emporium, Mysore for giving me access to their books and helping me compile illustrations

Mr. Arun Mehta for believing in the project and for ensuring that I never forget the reader in my creative frenzy

The brilliant art-team at Vakil & Sons Ltd., especially Mr. Sudhakar Tawde, Mr. Satish Nagvekar and Mrs. Rajeshree Sabnis, for their enthusiasm and support in transforming this book into reality

To Her, my *shakti*, may she always empower me

Thank You.

About this Book

Is God male or female?

Neither, say some religions. Male, say most. Female, say quite a few.

Hinduism makes room for all these beliefs. Sacred texts state that the divine principle is both *nirguna*, without form, and *saguna*, with form. As *nirguna*, the divine principle stands beyond the confines of gender. As *saguna*, God can be masculine or feminine. Hence the Shakta cult of the mother-goddess Devi is as important to the Hindu as the worship of Shiva and Vishnu.

Hinduism is one of the few surviving religions where the divine principle is adored in female form. No worship is complete without acknowledging Devi.

However, though aspects of the same divine principle, the way the Hindu devotee approaches Shiva and Vishnu is quite different from the way he approaches Devi. This is clear from the offerings made to the three deities.

The devotee offers Shiva uncooked vegetables and fruits and unprocessed milk. Such an offering befits the ascetic-god, who lives away from society on barren mountain tops. Vishnu receives rich buttery food flavoured with jaggery, since he is the householder-god, who revels in and ensures the wellbeing of the world. Offerings to Devi are quite different and varied. In temples where she stands as the demure consort — Gauri beside Shiva and Lakshmi beside Vishnu — she receives the same offering as her husband. But in Devi temples, where the goddess stands alone as Durga or Kali, the sacrifice of male animals such as fowls, rams and buffaloes are or were fairly common. Where blood sacrifices are frowned upon, symbolic sacrifices are made using pumpkins, gourds and coconuts. The goddess, especially her malevolent forms, is also offered sour and pungent foodstuffs like lemons and chillies. Another significant feature is that the goddess is often given clothes, cosmetics and jewellery. Such offerings of adornments are rarely made to a male deity.

This book explores these differences in rituals through imagery and narrative tradition. Pictures and stories of Hindu gods and goddesses reflect how Hindus perceive life. In images, Shiva is either the formless *linga* or the ash-smeared ascetic; in stories, he is the reluctant groom who the gods have to coax into marriage. In images, Vishnu is the charming god who bedecks himself with flowers, sandalpaste and gold; in stories, he battles demons, charms damsels and ensures harmony of the world-order by upholding cosmic law or *dharma*.

Shiva clearly embodies the world-renouncing principle of life while Vishnu embodies the world-affirming principle of life.

Devi is the world Shiva seeks to renounce and Vishnu is duty-bound to protect. It is she who makes Shiva the householder; it is she who bestows responsibility upon Vishnu and provides him with the means to fulfil that responsibility. Hence, she is identified as *Shakti* or energy that Brahma uses to create the world, *Prakriti* or Nature whose order is maintained by Vishnu, *Maya* or alluring delusion that Shiva seeks to break free from.

The world that is Devi can enchant or overwhelm us. When the devotee offers the goddess blood sacrifice, he is acknowledging her power to create life by destroying life. When he offers her sour and pungent food, he acknowledges the totality of her divine personality — the pleasant as well as the forbidding, the beneficial as well as the harmful. Through the offering of bridal finery, he ritually makes known his desire to see only her kind and maternal side.

The aim of this book is to bring together the tales associated with the myriad manifestations of Devi, weaving through it Shakta philosophy and Hindu worldviews. It discusses rituals, beliefs and customs that express Shakta culture and the relationship between goddess worship and woman's position in society. Also included is a chapter on mother-goddesses in foreign lands.

Despite a vast amount of research that has gone into obtaining the information and images compiled in this book, this book remains ultimately just an introduction, not an in-depth study of the Shakta tales and traditions. For those interested in a deeper understanding of the subject, there is a bibliography at the end of the book.

I hope and pray that my book successfully brings to light the games gods play to amuse and uplift man. And may it appease the almighty goddess.

— **Devdutt Pattanaik**

Shree Panchami, 2000

Within infinite myths lies the Eternal Truth.
Who sees it all?
Varuna has but a thousand eyes,
Indra has a hundred,
And I, only two.

Devi in her creative manifestation
bearing fertility symbols such as
sugarcane, lotus, conch-shell and
parrot; calendar print

Earliest Divinity

Her image has graced Stone Age caves. Her idols have stood in ancient temples. Hers was the first sacred form to be moulded by man.

In Japan, she was **Amaterasu**, the sun-goddess; in Greece, she was **Demeter**, the corn-goddess; in Egypt, she was **Isis**, the river-goddess. The Vikings called her **Frejya**, the Eskimos called her **Sedna**, the Romans called her **Artemis**. She was the Mexican **Coatlicue**, the Tibetan **Tara**, the Babylonian **Ishtar**, the Indian **Shakti**.

In every place she was the same: life-bestower, nourisher, lover, comforter, and final killer. She was the mother-goddess who resided in dark caves or sat on pink lotuses surrounded by birds and beasts, spinning the web of life and kneading the earth with life-giving sap.

Archaeological excavations across Europe and West Asia have revealed pre-historic paintings and carvings of women with exaggerated feminine features indicating the awe of the ancient artist with the life-giving capacity of woman. Some figures actually show women giving birth. The role of man in the creative process is spasmodic, momentary. It is the woman who nurtures the fetus in the womb and nourishes the newborn on the breast. She was therefore seen in early societies as an extension of the earth, another mysterious manifestation of cosmic fecundity.

In the rhythmic cycles of Nature — the rising and setting of the sun, the waxing and waning of the moon, the change of seasons, the dance of tides and the shifting fertility of women — man sensed the unending transformations of the goddess: from seductive nymph through tender matron to stern crone.

Domestication of the Wild Woman

So long as man lived in villages, in close touch with Nature, he understood the interplay of creative and destructive forces. He accepted the dynamism and diversity of the world around as the essence of the goddess.

But then he began migrating and moving into cities, trying to escape the vagaries of the natural world. Nature appeared more and more like a chaotic force to be mastered.

Mother-goddess bearing children, animals and plants in her arms; wood carving from Gujarat

Magna Mater: Mother of the universe; marble wall from ancient Rome

Such nomadic and urban thoughts made man turn away from the mother-goddess. He sought refuge in a wise, almighty father-god, a divine warrior who would restrain the wildness of Nature and domesticate it for the benefit of mankind.

And so the mother-goddess, until then free, was given a lord, a master, a husband. Marriage and maternity became tools to tame her.

Myths emerged of how powerful warrior gods forced wild goddesses into submission. In Babylon, bards narrated with relish the story of how Marduk killed the female monster Tiamat and created the earth out of her dead body. In Greece, the local goddesses of the plains and valleys were reduced to nymphs who the Olympian god Zeus seduced or raped.

Unattached, the mother-goddess was feared. Her powers were considered untamable, hence dangerous. She was invoked only to kill demons. But as the consort of a male god she was much more approachable. Her powers were checked and put to good use.

The wild goddess, who continued to dwell outside human settlements, was associated with disease, death and misfortune. She was warded away as a demoness or transformed into an ogress, to be despised by all.

This psychological shift was reflected in human society. Woman, worshipped for her ability to create new life, became a wife. Her freedom was curtailed. Her faithfulness was touted as the hallmark of all feminine virtue. She became subservient to her husband's will. Like the earth, she became man's property.

Rejection of the Temptress

A Stone Age icon of the mother-goddess from France with exaggerated feminine features

Around 600 B.C. there was another noticeable shift in human psyche — from world affirmation to world negation. It was the age that saw the rise of Buddhism in India and Orphism in Europe. No more was life exciting, worth exploring or enjoying. Instead the world was perceived as a mire of desire and delusions. The ageing body was seen as the prison of the blissful soul.

Man sought *moksha* — an escape from the vagaries of Nature, from the cycle of birth and death.

He rejected woman and sought refuge in monasteries. To him, woman was the temptress. She represented worldly life — children, family, responsibilities. She was the force that trapped the soul on earth.

Such beliefs led to further deterioration in the social status of women and the divine status of the mother-goddess. She became the root of evil, the cause of sorrow.

Ancient fertility rites such as blood sacrifices associated with the worship of the goddess were frowned upon. Her rituals were abandoned, her temples neglected. Her religion waned into twilight.

The Semites of Asia Minor and Arabia and the Aryans of Indo-Europe played a significant role in replacing the worship of the earth-mother with the worship of sky-gods. In the Bible, the patriarchs, instructed by the god of the Hebrews Yahweh, condemn the worship of **Ashtoreth**, love-goddess of Palestine. Vedic priests sang hymns to celebrate the triumph of the thunder-god Indra over **Ushas**, the dawn-goddess. Christian emperors of Byzantium shut down temples dedicated to the goddesses **Artemis** and **Isis**. When Islam was established in the seventh century, the worship of the goddess **Al-Lat** ceased in the cities of Mecca and Medina and became akin to blasphemy.

An ancient village-goddess; North Indian bronze

East and West

Both in the East and the West, earth-bound religions gave way to religions that gazed sky-wards. The procreative abilities of women were perceived as profane. Menstruation was associated with pollution and sickness, something to be ashamed of. Communities that once publicly celebrated the emergence of a child from the mother's womb, shunned the birthing rites. Sexual symbolism were no longer used to rouse the fertility of Nature; they aroused disgust.

Monks, who were mostly men, turned away the two principles that sustain Nature — sex and violence. Celibacy and non-violence became the means to break free from earthly bondage and to acquire powers that gave man powers over Nature itself. Violence was

Hera: Queen of Greek gods who had to endure the infidelity of her husband Zeus

3

Tree-nymph on a gateway built around a Buddhist Stupa in 400 A.D. in Central India

celebrated only when it helped impose the religion of the male gods.

Religions in the West and the East evolved differently.

The West saw life as a constant battle between good and evil, between materialism and spirituality. All that was undesirable came from the evil of the flesh. It had to be rejected in favour of the pure soul. The free, unattached, sensuous aspect of the goddess was associated with diabolical forces, with materialism, with evil. The mild, virginal, chaste aspect was linked to the divine, to the spirit, though she was never equated to the Supreme Divine Principle.

In the East, there were no absolutes: there was no absolute good and absolute evil. All that was undesirable came from ignorance; all that was desirable came from enlightenment. Life was an attempt to harmonise matter with spirit, the mother-goddess with the father-god. Man had the option to either relish the fleeting pleasures of worldly life with awareness or transcend it through realisation. Such an attitude allowed the mother-goddess cult to flourish, especially in India.

The Goddess in India

Two traditions evolved in India: the Vedic and the Tantrik.

Both linked the goddess to *samsara*, the manifest cycle of birth and rebirth, the material world, the realm of eternal change. She was the flow of energy, the substance that embodies the soul and gives form and identity to all. As **Shakti**, the goddess was supreme untamable universal energy. As **Shree**, she was the supreme domesticated goddess of fortune. She was **Maya**, the supreme unfathomable delusion of existence. She was **Prakriti**, Mother Nature, responsible for earthly existence. From her came material pleasures and worldly powers, *kama* and *artha*.

The male gods were more closely associated with unmanifest reality, pure consciousness, the still soul or *atma*. The ascetic Shiva sought *moksha*, liberation from material fetters, while the more worldly Vishnu propounded the doctrine of *dharma*, detached fulfilment of social obligations.

Thus the goddess and the god stood at two ends of the metaphysical spectrum. She represented material reality, he represented spiritual reality. Together, they gave life fullness and completeness.

In the Cities of the Indus

Cities dating 3000 years before the birth of Jesus have been excavated in many parts of Rajasthan, Gujarat, Punjab and in the valley of the Indus river that flows through what is now Pakistan. In these cities, archaeologists have found stones resembling the *yoni* or womb and one seal with the image of a woman giving birth to a tree. This has led to speculation that the religion of North India, before the Vedic culture came into the picture, was that of the mother-goddess. Crude figurines similar to the images of later-day village-goddesses have also been found lending credibility to this speculation.

Images of what is believed to be the mother-goddess have also been found in the Zhob and Kulli cultures of Baluchistan which predate the Indus valley civilization. The features of these images evoke terror and remind scholars of the Hindu goddess Kali.

All this has led many anthropologists to hypotheticize that ancient tribes and cities of India worshipped the earth-goddess before they were overwhelmed around 2000 B.C. by the Vedic ways of the militaristic and nomadic Aryans. Until the Indus script is deciphered, the truth may never be known.

Apsara: the celestial enchantress and water-nymph; stone carving from Central India

5

Devi in the *Vedas*

The Vedic culture was patriarchal and pedantic. In the Vedas, the earliest of Hindu holy books, the goddess was known as **Aditi**, the infinite one. She was presented as the mother of the powerful, chariot-riding, thunderbolt-weilding, ambrosia-drinking solar gods who conquered cities and put their enemies to shame. These warrior-gods were seen as masters of the universe and were invoked through ritual ceremonies known as *yagna*s. Hymns to their glory dominate the sacred texts and overshadow the presence of goddesses like **Ushas**, mistress of dawn and **Aranyani**, keeper of forests.

The *Brahmana*s or ritual texts presented intricate details of *yagna* to energise these powerful gods and help them subdue Nature's unwholesome side. In the forest texts or *Aranyaka*s, and later in the *Upanishads*, philosophies evolved that saw Nature as illusory and unworthy of attachment. In later Vedic lore, as a result, the awesome power of Devi was underplayed and her role as the shy and the submissive consort of the *deva* was celebrated.

Devi in the Tantra

The Tantrik culture drew on the power of the Devi. It evolved potent chants or *mantra*s, diagrams such as *mandala*s and *yantra*s, gestures called *mudra*s and vows known as *vrata*s, to make Nature bestow health, harvest and happiness. Such a culture probably flourished in the cities of the Indus valley and survived in the villages and tribes of India.

Women played a powerful role in these rituals for they were mediums through which Devi's grace percolated into society. Their presence was required to make every occasion auspicious. In spring festivals, women were asked to sing, dance and kick trees to accelerate their flowering and fruition.

This was the religion of the common man, of the farmer, the potter, the weaver, the tanner, the blacksmith and the forest-dweller.

The goddess of this religion was powerful, untamable, wild and free.

The Triumph of Devi

When the culture of *yagna*s was overwhelmed by Buddhism and Jainism around 500 B.C., Vedism was forced to adapt to ground realities.

In order to survive it accepted and adopted the beliefs and customs of the common man. It incorporated within its pantheon the rustic divinities of rural communities that

Goddess as consort of Brahma (top), Vishnu (middle) and Shiva (bottom); Tanjore Painting

6

included the awesome goddesses of the Tantrik tradition — **Tripurasundari, Mahamari, Chandika, Matrika, Bhairavi.**

Thus did Hinduism come into being, with old patriarchal Vedic gods being redefined to make room for powerful and popular mother-goddesses.

Shiva was enchanted into *samsara* by Devi, while Vishnu became responsible for her welfare. She was consort, mother and lover of male gods. Her passion was recognised and revered. She became Krishna's **Radha**, fiery and free, willing to throw caution to the winds, and meet her beloved on moonlit nights in fragrant meadows. She was also Rama's **Sita**, resolutely faithful to her husband.

The male trinity of Brahma, Vishnu and Shiva personified activity: creation, preservation and destruction. The female trinity of Saraswati, Lakshmi and Kali personified possessions: knowledge, wealth and power. The gods acted. The goddesses were acquired. There was a sort of objectification of the mother-goddess.

Devi was the embodiment of the universe, **Adi-Maya-Shakti**. Brahma, Vishnu and Shiva reacted to her splendour by celebrating, protecting or renouncing her.

Devi in Buddhism and Jainism

Neither Buddhism nor Jainism could not shy away from the power of Devi.

In Vajrayana Buddhism, the goddesses were accepted as keepers of knowledge, *prajna*, who embraced Buddhas, the embodiments of compassion, *karuna*. Together they conceived enlightenment for all. Practitioners of Tantrik

Shree-*yantra*: Abstract Tantrik art capturing the essence of Lakshmi, goddess of fortune

Buddhist goddesses: *Prajna*, keeper of knowledge, embracing the Buddha (left) and *Dakini* dancing (right); Tibetian bronze

7

Lakshmi massaging Vishnu's feet;
Pahari miniature

Buddhism invoked the *dakini*s, embodiments of Nature's secrets, to initiate them in the mysteries of the universe.

To the Jains, the goddess Shree was the source of auspiciousness and abundance who heralded the birth of *tirthankara* sages, *chakravarti* kings and mighty *baladeva* heroes. She was also worshipped as Ambika, mother of children and worldly joy. Jain artists visualized the universe as a woman from which the monks sought to liberate themselves.

Birth of Patriarchy

Vishnu and Shiva at Devi's feet;
wood carving from Orissa

In the forests, long before civilisation's stifling influence, ancient Indian tribes heard Devi's wild, unrestrained, virginal laughter. She was found residing in trees, with birds and beasts. She was **Bagalamukhi**, the heron-faced goddess. She was the turtle-riding **Yamuna** and the crocodile-riding **Ganga** — proud, turbulent river-goddesses. She belonged to all. She was **Renuka**, mistress of earth. She was **Yellamma**, everyone's mother.

But as man became the master, the owner, the lord, he fenced off the land, plucked away the weeds, seared the earth with a plough and sowed the seed of his choice. The earth became man's property, a field on which man harvested his fortune. Women, always equated with earth, were seen as fields too. Man was its jealous farmer. Thus was patriarchy born.

With the domestication of earth, Devi's wildness was rejected; she became the coy village-goddess, the *grama*-devi, whose chastity ensured the village fortune. Likewise, it was believed that a coy and chaste wife ensured the fortune of her husband.

8

Women in Hindu Society

When a new bride enters a Hindu household, conches are blown and drums are beaten. When she becomes pregnant, everybody gathers to celebrate her procreative ability. She is seen as the diminutive double of the goddess.

Without a woman by his side, no man can become a *grihapati*, master of the household. Without her, he cannot become *yajamana*, patron of ritual sacrifices. Just as matter is required to embody soul, man needs woman to raise a family and establish a home. She is therefore known as *sowbhagyavati*, bearer of good fortune.

Though her sacredness has always been acknowledged, every attempt was made to curtail feminine freedom. Her faithfulness to her husband became the hallmark of her virtue. Her chastity, it came to be believed, ensured happiness in the family. So much so that even when her husband died, she was expected to remain true to her husband's memory. Without her husband, she became a non-entity, an inauspicious widow. If she killed herself on his funeral pyre she was worshipped as a **Sati Maharani**. This practice of widows killing themselves on their husband's funeral pyre has been declared illegal by the Indian Government.

Though the goddess was the source of power, wealth and knowledge, Hindu women were denied the right to make decisions, the right to own property and the right to educate themselves. They were hidden behind veils, locked in the inner courtyard, trapped within thresholds, smothered by the alleged divinity of chaste wives and loving matriarchs.

Ambika: Goddess with a child in her arms; bronze idol from Bengal

Sati Maharani: the widow who kills herself on her husband's funeral pyre and becomes a goddess; calendar print

9

Worse still, they were seen as the fountainhead of temptation, hurdles on the path of spiritual progress, to be rejected by those who sought spiritual emancipation. They were the mythical *apsaras* who bewitched *rishis* and entrapped them in *samsara*. Many holymen avoided even casual contact with women lest they be tempted.

The paradoxical worship and suppression of women is perhaps the greatest tragedy in the mother-goddess cult within the Hindu fold.

Devi and Nationalism

It was the mother-goddess cult that spearheaded the quest for political liberation of the Indian people. The goddess manifested herself as Mother India in the writings of Bankim Chandra Chaterjee and provoked the people of India to take a stand against British imperialism. Images of **Maa Bharati** in chains roused the passion of a long suppressed people. Singing **Vande Mataram,** salutations to the mother, they revolted against foreign rule. The freedom struggle became a struggle to liberate the national goddess.

Through the ages, man has sought to either control or escape from the world around him. When both enterprises seem futile, he turns to the mother-goddess. And she offers him nourishment, strength, validation and unconditional love, so that man can come to terms with the world as it is, not as it should be. This, in essence, is the Shakta heritage.

Maa Bharati: the national goddess of modern India; calendar print

10

Durga's Triumph

Chapter II

Durga is the most splendid manifestation of Devi. Virginal and sublime, containing within her the power of all the gods combined, she is the invincible power of Nature who triumphs over those who seek to subjugate her.

This is her sacred narrative:

March of the Buffalo-demon

The buffalo-demon Mahisha stomped across the three worlds, kicking up dust, polluting earth and sea.

Neither Indra, king of the gods, nor Kumara, commander of celestial armies, could stop him. In despair, the gods turned to the cosmic guardian Vishnu for help. Vishnu confronted Mahisha, first as Narasimha, the man-lion, and then as Varaha, the boar, but each time he failed to subdue the demon.

Finally, Shiva, the supreme ascetic, disturbed by the pandemonium, opened his third eye and unleashed the fire of doom. But alas, even this dreaded missile, capable of destroying the three worlds, could not arrest Mahisha's march.

Durga: the warrior maiden; temple wall carving from Madhya Pradesh

Mahishasurmardini: killer of the buffalo demon; temple wall carving from Patan, Gujarat

Matrikas: Shaktis of gods; North
Indian stone carving

Vaishnavi, Kaumari, Aindri, Brahmi,
Varahi, Shivani, Narasimhi; North
Indian miniature painting

Rise of *Shaktis*

"Nothing can stop Mahisha now: he will soon control the universe and make Nature dance to his tunes," said Brahma, the creator.

"It will never be so; Nature can never be conquered." So saying, Brahma's divine strength, his *shakti*, emerged out of his body in the form of the goddess **Brahmi**. She rode a swan and held books of wisdom in her hands.

Simultaneously, the *shakti*s of the other gods emerged taking female forms.

From Indra, rose **Indrani** bearing a thunderbolt, riding an elephant; from Kumara, rose **Kaumari** holding a lance, riding a peacock; from Vishnu, rose **Vaishnavi** on an eagle with a discus whirring on her finger; from Narasimha, came **Narasimhi**, a raging lioness; from Varaha, came the sharp-tusked sow **Varahi**; from Shiva, came **Shivani** riding a bull bearing a trident.

Durga Manifests Herself

The seven *shakti*s, unrestrained by the bodies of the gods, were fearsome beings — the unbridled, untamed, restless energies of the cosmos. They would not submit to the authority of any man, beast or god, let alone a demon.

They rose into the sky and merged with each other in a blinding light. The sound of conches, drums and bells filled the air. With bated breath, the gods watched the spectacle unfolding before their eyes From the heavenly light rose a beautiful goddess: seductive yet serene, maternal yet forbidding.

"Who are you?" asked the gods.

"I am **Durga** — the inaccessible one, " replied the goddess. "I am **Prakriti**, the substance that gives form and identity to all things. I am **Shakti**, the power that enables

Durga seated on a lion;
contemporary marble statue

all creatures to exist, to feel, think, act and react. I am **Maya**, the delusion that makes life alluring yet elusive."

The gods saluted the great goddess. "Give me your weapons and I shall destroy he who seeks to dominate me," said Durga.

Shiva gave her his trident, Vishnu his discus and mace, Indra his thunderbolt, Kumara his lance, Brahma his bow. Then, mounting a lion, Durga prepared for battle.

Death of Shumbha and Nishumbha

Two demons, Shumbha and Nishumbha, saw the beautiful goddess standing atop Mount Meru. Overwhelmed by desire, they both sought her hand in marriage.

"I shall marry only one of you, the one who is stronger," said the goddess.

Durga facing Shumbha; Pahari miniature

"I am stronger," declared Shumbha. "No, it is I who am stronger," said Nishumbha.

To prove that the other was wrong, Shumbha and Nishumbha began fighting. Rocks were hurled, blows exchanged, until the two demons of equal strength ripped each other's hearts out and lay dead at Durga's feet.

13

Death of Chanda and Munda

News of **Vindhyavasini**, the beautiful goddess who resides atop a mountain, reached Mahisha. "She shall be my queen," declared the buffalo-demon. He ordered his generals, Chanda and Munda, to fetch her.

Chanda and Munda rushed to Mount Meru and placed Mahisha's offer of marriage before Durga.

When Durga did not reply, the demons threatened her with violence. The goddess responded by swinging her sword. In one sweep she cut off both their heads.

The gods named this amazing warrior-woman **Chandi**, the fierce one.

Armies of Mahisha

The violent rejection of his marriage proposal enraged Mahisha. "Bring that proud woman before me in chains. I shall teach her who is master."

A hundred thousand asuras armed with bows, arrows, spears and swords surrounded Mount Meru, determined to capture Durga. But as they marched up the hill, the goddess hurled her missiles. Before long, a hundred thousand demon heads were seen rolling down Mount Meru smearing its slopes red.

The goddess drank the blood of the demons. Then, seizing a lute and drum, she made music to celebrate her victory.

Devi with her attendants riding a chariot drawn by tigers; Pahari miniature

Durga attacking the buffalo-demon; relief from Kailasa temple, Ellora, Maharashtra

Death of Mahisha

Humiliated in defeat, Mahisha asked, "Why won't you marry me? Am I not lord of the three worlds?"

"I shall marry only he who defeats me in battle," revealed the goddess.

"Then let us fight."

A great battle commenced. Mountains shook, oceans trembled, clouds scattered across the sky, as the buffalo-demon attacked Durga. He rushed towards her, sometimes as a buffalo, sometimes as a lion, sometimes as an elephant. The goddess broke the buffalo's horns with her mace, sheared the lion's mane with her lance, cut the elephant's trunk with her sword.

Weapon after weapon, she hurled at the buffalo-demon, but each time he managed to rise up undefeated.

Realising that her weapons had no effect on Mahisha, Durga threw them aside, dismounted, and with her bare hands sprang upon Mahisha's back; with her tender feet she kicked his head.

The demon — immune to the weapons of all the gods — fell senseless at the touch of Durga's feet.

Durga then raised her trident and plunged it into the buffalo-demon's heart.

Devi's Splendour

The gods descended from their celestial abode, saluting Durga, praising her valour. From beneath the earth rose the forest spirits, *yaksha*s and *naga*s. They offered the goddess flowers, incense and jewellery. Sages venerated her with lamps.

Durga killing Mahisha; bronze from Himachal Pradesh

15

Devi riding a tiger; modern calendar print

"Stay with us, protect us, do not leave us," they cried.

Said the goddess, "I am always with you. I am the mother who feeds you, the sister who supports you, the daughter who charms you, the nymph who enchants you.

"I am **Saraswati** who bestows upon Brahma the knowledge to create the world; I am **Lakshmi** who gives Vishnu the wherewithal to preserve the cosmic order; I am **Parvati** who allures the ascetic Shiva into worldly life.

"I am the heat of fire, the movement of wind, the moisture of water, the radiance of suns, the lustre of moons, the sparkle of stars, the fecundity of soil, the sovereignty of kings.

"I am **Prithvi**, the sacred earth, bringing forth life, nurturing all plants and animals. I am *grama-devi*, the village goddess, on whose body man builds houses and grows crops.

"My essence is present in every woman. They, like me, are vessels of fertility, sources of love and life."

Chamundi: killer of demons Chanda and Munda; Mysore painting

16

Saraswati's Wisdom

Saraswati, goddess of knowledge and the arts, embodies the wisdom of Devi. She is the river of consciousness that enlivens creation. She is the dawn-goddess, whose rays dispels the darkness of ignorance. Without her, there is only chaos and confusion. To realise her one must go beyond the pleasures of the senses and rejoice in the serenity of the spirit.

This is her sacred narrative:

Eyes of Wisdom

In the beginning, there was chaos: everything existed in a formless fluid state. "How do I bring order to this disorder?" wondered Brahma, the creator.

"With knowledge," said Devi. Heralded by a peacock, sacred books in one hand and a lute in the other, dressed in white, she emerged from Brahma's mouth riding a swan as the goddess Saraswati.

Said the goddess, "Knowledge helps man find possibilities where once he saw problems."

By her grace, Brahma acquired the power to sense, think, comprehend and communicate. He began looking upon chaos with eyes of wisdom and saw the wonderful potential therein.

Saraswati, goddess of knowledge and the arts; Mysore painting

The Power of Sound

Brahma discovered the melody of *mantra*s in the cacophony of chaos. In his joy, he named Saraswati **Vagdevi**, goddess of speech and sound.

The sound of *mantra*s filled the universe with vital energy, *prana*. Things began to take shape and the cosmos acquired a structure: the sky dotted with stars rose to form the heavens, the sea sank into the abyss below, the earth stood in between.

Gods became lords of the celestial spheres, demons ruled the nether regions, humans walked on earth. The sun rose and set, the moon waxed and waned, the tide flowed and ebbed. Seasons changed, seeds germinated, plants bloomed and withered, animals migrated and reproduced, as randomness gave way to the rhythm of life.

Brahma thus became the creator of the world with Saraswati as his wisdom.

Brahma and Saraswati; embroidery from Gujarat

Four-headed Brahma, the creator of the universe; stone carving

Brahma's Infatuation

Saraswati was the first being to come into Brahma's world. Brahma looked upon her with eyes of desire. She turned away saying, "All I offer must be used to elevate the spirit, not indulge the senses."

But Brahma could not control his amorous thoughts; he continued staring at Saraswati. He gave himself four heads facing the four cardinal directions so that he could look upon Saraswati at all times.

Saraswati moved away from Brahma, taking the form of a cow. Brahma followed her as a bull. Saraswati then changed into a mare; Brahma pursued her as a horse. Every time Saraswati turned into a bird or a beast — be it a goose or a doe — Brahma became the corresponding male — a gander, then a buck — determined to possess her. But no matter how hard he tried, he could not catch her.

The goddess with multiple forms came to be known as **Shatarupa**. She personified material reality, alluring yet fleeting.

Saraswati Curses Brahma

Angered by his display of unbridled passion, Saraswati cursed Brahma, "You have filled the world with longing that is the seed of unhappiness. You have fettered the soul in the flesh. You are not worthy of reverence. May there be hardly any temple or festival in your name."

So it came to pass that there are only two temples of Brahma in India: one at Pushkar, Rajasthan and another at Kumbhakonam, Tamil Nadu.

Undaunted by the curse, Brahma continued to cast his lustful looks upon Saraswati. He gave himself a fifth head to enhance his gaze.

Bhairava; tribal stone carving from Madhya Pradesh

Bhairava Confronts Brahma

Brahma's action motivated by desire confined consciousness and excited the ego. It disturbed the serenity of the cosmos and roused Shiva, the supreme ascetic, from his meditation.

Shiva opened his eyes, sensed Saraswati's discomfort and in a fit of rage turned into Bhairava, lord of terror. His eyes were red, his growl menacing. He lunged towards Brahma and with his sharp claws, wrenched off Brahma's fifth head. The violence subdued Brahma's passion.

Brahma's cut head, however, seared through Bhairava's flesh and clung to Bhairava's hand, sapping him of all vitality, driving him mad. The lord of terror ranted and raved, losing all control of his senses.

The goddess, pleased with Bhairava's timely action, rushed to his rescue. With her gentle touch she nursed him as a child, restored his sanity and accepted him as her companion and guard.

Brahma, sobered by his encounter with Bhairava, sought a way out from the labyrinth of desires. The goddess Saraswati revealed to him the doctrine of liberation.

Savitri's Ire

Brahma decided to conduct a *yagna*. But a man without a wife can conduct no ritual. So he went to Saraswati and requested her to be his spouse and sit by him during the ceremony.

"I will be **Savitri**, your divine consort," said Saraswati. "But first I must bathe and prepare myself."

While Saraswati was away bathing, Brahma made preparations for the great *yagna*. He set up the altar, collected the sacred utensils, the wood, the flowers and fruits. Then he waited for Saraswati to return.

Hours passed. There was no sign of her. Hours turned into days, months and years.

Brahma's patience wore out. "I cannot wait for Savitri any more. I shall find another woman to assist me during the yagna." Brahma looked around and found a beautiful milkmaid. He passed her through the body of a cow and transformed her into a radiant goddess called **Gayatri**.

When Savitri returned and found Brahma making oblations into the sacred fire with another woman by his side, she was furious. She turned into a river and washed away the sacred altar.

Later when she calmed down, Savitri became one with Gayatri and helped Brahma conclude his *yagna* successfully.

Sublime Goddess

Saraswati wore neither jewels on her body nor painted herself with bright colours. Her white sari reflected her essential purity, her rejection of all that is base and materialistic.

She transcended the cravings of the flesh and rejoiced in the powers of the mind as the patron of pure wisdom. She came to embody all that is pure and sublime in Nature, untouched by passion.

The four Vedas, books of universal knowledge, were her offspring. Her mount, the swan, came to personify

Gayatri, the radiant goddess, born of a cow; calendar print

Brahma and Saraswati at one of the few temples dedicated to Brahma at Pushkar, Rajasthan

19

Saraswati with her lute and swan; contemporary idol from Bengal

Saraswati with her lute; Kalighat painting

pure knowledge and her herald, the peacock, became symbol of the arts.

Schools and libraries were her temples; books, pens, artistic tools and musical instruments were the ritualistic emblems of her worhsip. Those who worshipped her were blessed with the light of knowledge that drove away the demons of ignorance and unhappiness.

Asuras Reject Saraswati

Once when the *deva*s conducted a *yagna*, their arch enemies, the *asura*s, demanded a share of the sacrifice. Bound by the laws of hospitality, the *deva*s gave them the goddess Saraswati.

"Knowledge increases sorrow, speech leads to quarrels," said the *asura*s, rejecting the gift.

This angered Saraswati who decreed that while *deva*s would be the gods of wisdom, the *asura*s would be the demons of ignorance.

Slip of the Tongue

A demon practised many austerities to appease Brahma. Fearing that he may ask a boon that would make him invincible, the gods sought the help of the goddess Saraswati. The goddess sat on the tongue of the demon so that when it was time to ask for a boon all he could say was, "I would like to never stay awake."

"So be it," said Brahma.

As a result, the demon who wanted to conquer the three worlds, ended up going to sleep, forever.

Song of the *Gandharva*

The *gandharva*s were demigods who sprang from the fragrance of flowers. Once they stole the Soma plant whose inebriating and invigorating sap was much sought by the *deva*s. Its theft made the gods very unhappy.

Saraswati promised to recover the Soma plant. She went to the garden of the *gandharva*s and with her *veena* created enchanting tunes: the *raga*s and the *ragini*s.

"Give us this music," begged the *gandharva*s.

"Only if you give back the Soma plant to the *deva*s," said the goddess.

The *gandharva*s returned the Soma plant and learnt music from Saraswati. In time, they became celestial musicians whose melodies had more power to rouse the mind than any intoxicant.

Saraswati: goddess of learning and
arts seated on a lotus with her swan;
contemporary painting

21

Lakshmi and Saraswati

Brahma created the universe with the help of Saraswati.
Vishnu was the guardian of the cosmos. He too needed
Saraswati's support to sustain the cosmos. Using her
knowledge, he instituted and maintained *dharma*, sacred
laws that ensure stability and growth in society.

Vishnu also needed the help of Lakshmi, goddess of
wealth, who gave him the wherewithal to ensure
cosmic order.

The question arose: who did Vishnu need more? Lakshmi
or Saraswati? Wealth or knowledge? The goddesses
argued. "Knowledge does not fill an empty stomach," said
Lakshmi. "Wealth keeps man alive but gives no meaning
to life," said Saraswati.

"I need both knowledge and wealth to sustain the cosmos.
Without knowledge, I cannot plan. Without wealth,
I cannot implement a plan. Wealth sustains life; the arts
give value to life. Thus both Saraswati and Lakshmi are
needed to live a full life."

Vishnu, the preserver of the world,
with Lakshmi to his right and
Saraswati to his left; North Indian
stone carving

Brahma, Vishnu and Shiva adoring
Saraswati, goddess of learning;
Pahari miniature

Mare of Doom

Shiva, the destroyer, once opened his third eye.
Out came a terrible fire that threatened to burn the
three worlds.

There was panic everywhere. Only Saraswati remained
calm. "Shiva's fire burns only that which is impure and
corrupt," she said.

She took the form of a river and with her pure waters
picked up the dreaded fire. She carried it gently far away
from the earth into the bottom of the sea where it
transformed into a fire-breathing mare called Badavagni
— the beast of doom.

"So long as the world is pure and man wise, this terrible
creature will remain on the bottom of the sea. But when
wisdom is abandoned and man corrupts the world,
Badavagni will emerge and destroy the universe,"
said Saraswati.

The *devas* and the *asuras* saluted Saraswati whose wisdom
and purity had saved the world from Shiva's fury.

From that day, Saraswati came to be seen as the
fountainhead of knowledge, **Sharda**, who leads man from
darkness to light, from ignorance to enlightenment, from
material decadence to spiritual upliftment.

Aum bhur bhuvah svahah
Tat savitur varenyum
Bhargo devasya dheemahee
Dhiyo yo nah prachodayat

May the resplendent divine who is
the life breath of the universe, who
pervades the three worlds, who removes
miseries, brings joy, dispels darkness
and ignorance, propel my intelligence in
the right direction

(The hymn that is the goddess Gayatri)   23

Bhoodevi being raised by the divine
boar from the bottom of the sea;
24   Mysore painting

Lakshmi's Bounty

Lakshmi — goddess of affluence and abundance — represents the beautiful and bountiful aspect of Nature. As Bhoodevi, the earth-goddess, she nurtures life; as Shreedevi, the goddess of fortune, she bestows power, pleasure and prosperity on those who deserve her grace. To realise her, one must respect the laws of life and appreciate the wonders of existence.

This is her sacred narrative:

Prajapati Raises the Earth

In the beginning, there was water everywhere. There was nothing to eat, nowhere to live. Prajapati, the divine patriarch, father of the gods and demons, saw the plight of his children and invoked Devi.

The goddess whispered into his ear, "The earth lies trapped under the water. Raise it up."

Prajapati took the form of a mighty boar called Emusha, plunged into the sea and found the earth-goddess **Bhoodevi** on the ocean floor. Placing her on his snout, he gently raised her to the surface.

Prajapati then turned into Akupara, a giant turtle, and offered Bhoodevi a seat on his back.

Shreedevi Favours Bali

Seated on the celestial turtle, the earth-goddess nurtured life in her bountiful arms. She offered food and shelter to all.

The *deva*s admired her beauty; the *asura*s craved her wealth. They fought many a battle over her. Finally, under the leadership of Bali, the *asura*s emerged triumphant.

Impressed by Bali's strength, the goddess came to him as **Shreedevi** and crowned him king of the earth. She offered him a throne, a footstool and held a parasol over his head.

Shreedevi's sacred white elephants turned into clouds and sprinkled life-bestowing rain upon the earth, watering fields and pastures, so that crops grew abundantly and cows gave plenty of milk. Everyone was happy with Bali as their king.

Vishnu's Three Steps

Power made Bali arrogant. He declared, "The earth belongs to me; I can give anyone anything he desires."

Chapter IV

Lakshmi, goddess of affluence and abundance; calendar print

Bhoodevi as the goddess of grain; bronze idol from Andhra Pradesh

These words annoyed the earth-goddess: she belonged to nobody and certainly was not a commodity to be given away as a gift.

Indra, leader of the *deva*s, meanwhile, bereft of Shreedevi's grace had been reduced to poverty. He approached Bali and begged for some land. To mock him, Bali pointed to Vishnu, the shortest of the gods, and said, "I shall give you as much land as this little one can cover in three strides."

As soon as Bali said this, Vishnu began to grow in size; he turned into a giant who strode across and claimed all of Bali's kingdom in two steps. With his third step, Vishnu shoved Bali into the nether region.

Vishnu thus wrested control of the earth for the gods.

The Fickle One

"The gods may lack strength, but they are intelligent. I shall go to them." So saying Shreedevi turned away from Bali and went to the gods. She blessed the gods with ruling majesty, material prosperity, physical health, bodily beauty and divine fortune.

Angry and bitter in defeat, the demons rasped, "Shreedevi is **Chanchala**, the fickle one. Once she favoured Bali; now she favours Indra. She is faithful to none."

"That is not true," said the goddess, "I am eternally faithful to he who does not abuse my gifts."

Vishnu's Detachment

Vishnu, who had conquered the earth for the gods, let Indra become king.

"Don't you want to be lord of the universe and enjoy the splendours of the cosmos?" asked Shreedevi.

"I desire nothing. By defeating the demon Bali, I have done my duty. I seek no reward for it."

These words of Vishnu pleased Shreedevi.

Indra Angers Bhoodevi and Shreedevi

The goddess said, "He who takes good care of the earth-goddess Bhoodevi, wins the affection of Shreedevi, goddess of fortune, and becomes king of the cosmos."

But Indra did not heed her words. Soon after being crowned king, the leader of the *deva*s retired to the pleasure gardens. He drank wine, enjoyed song and dance and neglected his royal duties.

The earth, left ungoverned, was plundered.

Lakshmi in her warrior manifestation riding an owl; North Indian sculpture

Bhoodevi's lamentations fell on deaf ears. This made Shreedevi very angry. She turned away from Indra.

Shreedevi Disappears

"Wealth and power corrupted the demon-king. Now, pleasure and comfort has weakened the god-king. Neither holds on to *dharma* for long. Neither deserves my grace." So saying, the goddess dissolved herself in the ocean of milk.

Instantly a gloom descended upon the world: it no longer reverberated with song and dance. Weapons lost their power, gems their sparkle, men their vigour. Cows did not give milk, fields became barren, trees bore neither flower nor fruit. The cosmos became a desolate place, bereft of joy and laughter.

Churning of the Ocean

The goddess's disappearance caused panic in three worlds.

"We must bring her back," said the gods.

"But how?" wondered the demons.

"By churning the ocean of milk," said Vishnu.

With Mandara, king of mountains, as the spindle and Akupara, king of turtles, as the base, the *deva*s and the *asura*s created the cosmic churn. Using Vasuki, the king of serpents, as the churning rope, they began churning the ocean of milk.

Indra, the king of Gods; wood carving from Kerala

Churning of the ocean; contemporary illustration

Rise of Lakshmi from the ocean of
milk; Tanjore painting

Lakshmi Rises

The churn twisted and turned, the ocean frothed and
fumed, waves roared and spewed foam in every direction.
Aeons passed. Nothing emerged. But the gods and
demons, determined to bring the goddess back, continued
to churn.

Pleased by their efforts, the goddess finally emerged as
Lakshmi, the desirable one, in all her splendour.

Seated on a dew-drenched lotus, dressed in red silk,
bedecked in gold, she was the very embodiment of
affluence, abundance and auspiciousness.

As she rose, *rasa*, life giving sap, began flowing in every
direction. The earth palpated with life. Joy filled the air.

The gods saluted her, the demons sang songs to her glory.

Sacred elephants who hold up the sky came from the
eight quarters of the universe, raised their trunks and
consecrated her with life-sustaining water.

Namastestu mahaamaaye
Shripeethe surapoojite,
Shankhachakragadaahaste
Sri Mahaalakshmi namostute

Salutations, divine enchantment,
Seat of auspiciousness,
Who is adored by the gods,
Bearer of a conch, discus and mace.
Salutations to you,
Great goddess of affluence and
abundance.

Gifts of Prosperity

With Lakshmi came a cow called Kamadhenu with
enough milk to feed the world for all eternity, a wish-
fulfilling gem called Chintamani and a tree called
Kalpataru that bore every flower and fruit desirable.

In her hand she held the basket of bounty: the Akshaya Patra overflowing with grain and gold.

Lakshmi revealed to Kubera, lord of the forest spirits called *yaksha*s the locations of minerals, gems and secret treasures. She made *naga*s, the serpents, the keepers of earth's fertility.

From her being emerged her seven daughters, the sacred river-goddesses **Ganga**, **Yamuna**, **Sindhu**, **Narmada**, **Godavari**, **Krishna** and **Kaveri** who nourished the earth and supported life.

Kamadhenu: cow of prosperity; calendar image

Gifts of Pleasure

With Lakshmi came Kama, the delightful god of pleasure. Riding his parrot, surrounded by bees and butterflies, this handsome god raised his sugarcane bow and shot arrows dripping with desire into the heart of every being. He roused the senses, excited the mind, inspired the heart.

With Kama came Priti and Rati, goddesses of love and longing, and Vasanta, lord of spring. Wherever they went, flowers bloomed to welcome them with offerings of nectar and pollen. Bees buzzed, birds sang songs of love, and animals danced.

Behind Lakshmi stood Rambha, the beautiful nymph who knew sixty-four ways to pleasure the senses, and Sura, the goddess of intoxicants, who could soothe tired nerves and enchant the mind with dreams.

Rambha: the nymph who provides pleasure; stone sculpture from Gujarat

Gifts of Power

Along with Lakshmi came the six-tusked, white-skinned elephant Airavata and the seven-headed flying horse Ucchaishrava. The gods claimed the elephant, the demons, the horse.

The goddess also brought forth a throne, a crown, a footstool, a parasol, a fly-whisk, a cushion, a fan, a bow and a conch. "These symbols of kingship," she said, "will go to a worthy being, one who will use power to preserve and protect life."

"Give them to me," said Indra, king of the gods.

"No, you are too obsessed with pleasure," said Lakshmi.

"Give them to me," said Bali, king of the demons.

"No, wealth corrupts you and makes you arrogant."

Lakshmi sought someone who would not succumb to the allure of power, pleasure and prosperity; someone strong, wise and virtuous, capable of using force, charm and guile with discretion to uphold the laws of life.

She chose Vishnu.

Lakshmi at Vishnu's feet in the form of a domesticated and docile wife; Rajasthani wall painting

Lakshmi Marries Vishnu

Lakshmi placed Vaijayanati, the fragrant garland of victory, round Vishnu's neck and made him her consort. He became known as Shreenatha, beloved of fortune.

Vishnu placed Shreevasta, the symbol of Lakshmi, on his chest.

Their abode, Vaikuntha, became the pivot of the cosmos.

Vishnu battled the forces of chaos and corruption and diligently performed his duties as guardian of the world, pleasing Lakshmi, who rewarded him with her love and affection, tending to his every need like a devoted wife.

Every time Vishnu returned to Vaikuntha, tired after his battle with the demons, the goddess invigorated him with her affectionate touch.

Vishnu with Shreedevi and Bhoodevi; South Indian bronze

Birth of Alakshmi

Along with Lakshmi, rose Alakshmi, the goddess of barrenness and misfortune, from the ocean of milk. She was ugly with matted hair, sunken cheeks, shrivelled breasts and coarse limbs.

Said the goddess, "Lakshmi will dwell where there is nobility and righteousness, cleanliness and beauty, virtue and compassion. Alakshmi will dwell elsewhere, attracted by sloth, envy, greed, lust and pride."

And so it is that people who wish to keep Alakshmi away, keep their houses clean, their bodies beautiful and their minds pure.

Bhoodevi Runs Away

The earth-goddess Bhoodevi nourished all mankind with her bounty. Venerated by sages and seers, she belonged to all.

But man sought to possess her and plunder her wealth. Enraged, the goddess refused to let seeds sprout and plants bear fruit.

Mankind starved. Moved by the plight of man, Vishnu descended upon earth as the patriarch Prithu and tried to make peace with Bhoodevi. But the earth-goddess refused to forgive man; she ran away in the form of a cow.

Prithu pursued her on his chariot and threatened her with his arrows.

"If you harm me, the world will cease to be," warned Bhoodevi.

"I do not wish to harm you; I want you to feed mankind," said Prithu.

"Why should I nurture those who do not respect me?"

"Fear not. I shall make sure man respects the earth-mother and relates to her as a calf to a cow. I will be Gopala, your cowherd, protecting you from danger."

Vishnu, the protector with Lakshmi, the provider; calendar art

Bhoodevi Becomes Prithvi

And so it came to pass, Prithu instituted the practice of prudent economics and taught mankind how to draw on the earth's resources without exploiting her.

He also established the sacred laws of *dharma*, that ensure the stability in society, and maintains a harmonious relationship between man and the world around.

Pleased with this, Bhoodevi called herself Prithvi, beloved of Prithu.

Go-mata: earth-goddess in the form of a cow being chased by Prithu; Pahari painting

31

Vishnu Protects Bhoodevi

Vishnu became the blue sky who constantly watches over the red earth — Lakshmi herself. He ensured *dharma* was respected by all.

Once, the earth-goddess Bhoodevi appeared before Vishnu in the form of a cow and said, "The ambitions of kings burdens my back. Their greed has made my udders sore. Save me, before they destroy me."

Vishnu immediately descended upon earth as the sage Parashurama, the prince Rama, the cowherd Krishna and killed the many wicked kings of earth who troubled the goddess. He then reestablished *dharma*.

Lakshmi was the provider; Vishnu was the protector. Together they formed the foundation of life.

Vishnu, the protector, with Lakshmi, the provider, forming the foundation of life; calendar print

Goddess of Compassion

Manu, the first man, once gave into desire at the cost of his duty, angering Vishnu, the stern keeper of cosmic laws.

Fearing divine retribution, Manu turned to Lakshmi, the tender half of the divine couple. And she, like a mother intervening between father and son, approached Vishnu and appealed for clemency. Vishnu, softened by Lakshmi's arguments, looked upon man with eyes of compassion.

And the world rejoiced.

Lakshmi, the goddess of beauty and bounty, thus became the goddess of mercy, who understood human frailties and accepted man despite all his shortcomings. It is to her man turns as he seeks clemency, love and favour.

White elephants, symbol of fertility and strength, saluting Lakshmi; miniature painting

Parvati's Love

Kali is the dark half of the Nature, the blood-thirsty malevolent mistress of death; Gauri is the bright side, the loving, tender, benevolent, keeper of life. Between them lies the mysteries of existence, the eternal flux of creation and destruction. As Sati-Parvati, the mother-goddess invites everyone into the cycle of life, helping each one come to terms with the unending transformations of *samsara*.

This is her sacred narrative:

Pillar of Fire

Shiva saw no sense in the transitory pleasures of life. So he rejected *samsara*, smeared his body with ash, closed his eyes and performed austerities.

Shiva's *tapas* generated so much heat that his body turned into a pillar of fire — a blazing *lingam* that threatened to destroy the whole world. The gods did not know how to control Shiva's fire.

Suddenly there appeared a *yoni* — the divine vessel of the mother-goddess. It caught the fiery *lingam* and contained its heat, thus saving the cosmos from untimely destruction.

Parvati; South Indian bronze

A Wife for Shiva

The gods realised that so long as Shiva remained an ascetic, aloof from worldly life, he would be a threat to all existence. "Some one must distract him from his *tapas* and make him appreciate the wonder of life," they said.

They requested Shiva to take a wife. "Who will marry me?" said Shiva. "Is there anyone in the cosmos who can withstand the power of my *tapas*? Find such a woman and I will marry her."

Chinnamastika; calendar print

Chinnamastika

The gods invoked the mother-goddess. She appeared before them as **Chinnamastika** — a headless goddess wearing a garland of skulls. In one hand she held a bloody sword, in the other was her cut head drinking blood that spurted from her severed neck. Under her feet lay a couple locked in passionate embrace.

Her appearance terrified the gods.

"Fear not, I am the power that produces life by consuming death," said Chinnamasta. "I shall charm Shiva and make him part of the material world."

Sati and Shiva; Pahari miniature painting

Daksha's Daughter

The goddess took birth as **Uma**, the daughter of Daksha, and declared her love for Shiva as soon as she was born.

Daksha was the priest-king of the cosmos who had laid down the rules of civilisation. He did not want his daughter to marry a mendicant who held worldly life in disdain.

Much against Daksha's wishes, Uma abandoned the comforts of society and went into the forest where she performed *tapa*s more terrible than the ones performed by any ascetic.

Sati and Shiva

Shiva was forced to acknowledge Uma's suitability as his bride. He let her be his companion.

Uma followed Shiva wherever he went, into cremation grounds, across desolate plains, over stark mountains, never complaining, never demanding, content just to be by his side. She became known as **Sati**, the perfect wife.

As the days passed, Shiva learnt to appreciate Sati's forbearance. He fell in love.

Daksha's Grand *Yagna*

Daksha meanwhile made preparations for a grand *yagna*. Everyone was invited to the ceremony, everyone except Shiva.

"Shiva does not respect the rules of society, behaves like a savage, makes no distinction between the sacred and the profane and wanders aimlessly in unholy lands. He does not deserve a share of this sacrifice," said Daksha.

Sati kills herself in the fire-altar; calendar print

Sati Kills Herself

When Sati learnt how her father intended to display his contempt for Shiva and his mendicant ways, she was most upset. Shiva tried to calm her down, but Sati refused to swallow the insult: her eyes turned red, her nostrils flared.

"I shall disrupt the *yagna* where my lord Shiva is not welcome," swore Sati.

She spat on the ground; out came ten fierce goddesses — the **Mahavidyas**, keepers of occult secrets who rushed into Daksha's sacrificial hall, cackling in fury. They broke the sacred utensils, ripped the tapestries, burnt the pavilion, spoiled the food, drove out all the assembled guests and frightened away the priests.

Sati then leapt into the fire-altar and burnt herself to death. With the sacred precinct contaminated by his daughter's blood, Daksha could not proceed with the *yagna*.

Shiva's Sorrow

When news of Sati's death reached Shiva, such was his fury that the earth shook and the sky trembled. Shiva turned into Bhairava, the lord of terror, raised his trident and lopped Daksha's pompous head off.

After the anger came the sorrow.

Shiva picked up the charred remains of Sati's corpse from Daksha's sacrificial altar, but could not bring himself to part with it. He placed it on his shoulders and began wandering across the cosmos, howling in agony.

Destruction of Sati's Corpse

"Behold Shiva," said the gods, "He who once abandoned the worldly pleasures now bemoans his beloved, suffering the pangs of existence. Love for Sati has made him part of *samsara*."

Shiva could not restrain his sorrow, so much so that his grief threatened to engulf the world.

So Vishnu, the guardian of the cosmos, hurled his discus and cut Sati's corpse into 108 pieces. These fell on Jambudvipa, the rose-apple continent of India.

Om sarvamangalamangalye
Shive sarvaarthasaadhike
Sharanye Triyambake Gauri
Naaraayani namostute

Adorations to the goddess
Who is the auspiciousness of all that is auspicious,
Who is the eternal consort of Shiva.
Adorations to you O three-eyed, fair goddess,
I have taken refuge in you.

Vishnu cutting Sati's corpse; contemporary illustration

35

Taraka Conquers Heaven

With Sati's corpse gone, Shiva isolated himself into a dark cave buried amongst snow covered peaks of the Himalayas. He rejected the world outside.

Meanwhile, the demons, led by Taraka, rose from the netherworld and drove the *deva*s out of the heavens. The gods sought a warrior who would help them regain the celestial realm.

"Only Shiva can father such a warrior," informed Brahma.

But Shiva, immersed in meditation, was oblivious to the problems of the gods. As he performed *tapas* his mind was filled with great knowledge and his body became resplendent with energy. But all this knowledge and energy, bottled within his being, was of no use to world at large.

Birth of Parvati

The gods, invoked the mother-goddess, who appeared before them as **Kundalini**, a coiled serpent.

"I will uncoil myself round Shiva, wean out his knowledge and energy for the good of the world and make him father a child," said Shakti.

Shakti took birth as **Parvati**, daughter of Himavan, lord of the mountains, determined to draw Shiva out of his cave and make him her consort.

Rati, goddess of longing holding a sugarcane; wood carving from Tamil Nadu

Priti and Rati

Every day, Parvati would visit Shiva's cave, sweep the floor, decorate it with flowers and offer him fruits, hoping to win his love.

But Shiva never opened his eyes to look upon her charming face. Exasperated, the goddess invoked **Priti** and **Rati**, goddesses of love and longing, to rouse Shiva out of his meditation.

These goddesses entered Shiva's desolate cave and transformed it into a pleasure-garden filled with the fragrance of flowers and the buzzing of bees.

Death of Kama

Guided by Priti and Rati, Kama, the lord of desire, raised his sugarcane bow and shot arrows dripping with desire into the heart of Shiva.

Shiva was not amused. He opened his third eye and released the flames of fury that engulfed Kama and reduced his beautiful body to ashes.

Shiva killing Kama and Rati mourns this tragedy; Pahari miniature painting

The death of Kama alarmed the gods. "Without the lord of desire, man will not embrace woman and life will cease to be."

Said Parvati, "I shall find another way to conquer Shiva's heart. When Shiva becomes my consort, Kama will be reborn."

Not Even a Leaf

Parvati went into the forest and performed rigorous *tapas*, wearing nothing to protect her tender body from the harsh weather, eating nothing, not even a leaf, earning the admiration of forest ascetics who named her **Aparna**.

Aparna matched Shiva in her capacity to cut herself from the world and completely master her physical needs. The power of her *tapas* shook Shiva out of his meditation. He stepped out of his cave and accepted Parvati as his wife.

Shiva married Parvati in the presence of the gods following the sacred rites and took her to the highest peak of the cosmos, Mount Kailasa, the pivot of the universe.

As the world revolved all around them, the two became one and Kama was reborn.

Hermit to Householder

Parvati melted Shiva's stern heart with her affection. Together they played dice on Mount Kailas or sported on the banks of lake Manasarovar, discovering the joys of married life.

The goddess awakened Shiva's concern for the world by questioning him on various issues. As he spoke, he

Parvati performing penance; North Indian sculpture

37

Shiva's wedding procession;
Kalamkari print from Andhra
Pradesh

revealed the secrets of the Tantras and the Vedas that he had gathered in aeons of meditation.

Inspired by her beauty, Shiva became the fountainhead of the arts, of dance and drama. He sang and danced to the delight of the gods who were pleased to see his enchantment with the goddess.

Celestial Warlord

Parvati gave Shiva's aura to the gods. "From this will rise the warlord you seek," said the goddess.

Shiva and Parvati; North Indian
stone carving

The gods gave Shiva's aura to **Svaha**, consort of Agni, the fire-god. Unable to bear its heat for long, she gave it to Ganga, the river goddess, who cooled it in her icy waters until it turned into a seed.

Aranyani, the goddess of the forest, embedded the divine seed in the fertile forest floor where it was transformed into a robust child with six heads and twelve arms.

Six forest nymphs called the **Krittikas** found this magnificent child in a lotus. Overcome by maternal affection, they began nursing him. The six-headed son of Shiva, born of many mothers, came to be known as Kartikeya.

Parvati taught Kartikeya the art of war and turned him into the celestial warlord called Skanda.

Skanda took command of the celestial armies, defeated Taraka in battle and restored the heavens to the gods.

38

Kali Drinks Raktabija's Blood

Skanda, guardian of the heavens, went on to destroy many demons who opposed the reign of the gods.

But he could not defeat the demon Raktabija. Whenever this demon's blood touched the ground, a thousand new demons sprang to life. He seemed invulnerable.

To aid her helpless son, Parvati entered the cosmic battlefield as the dreaded goddess Kali — dark as death, gaunt with sunken eyes, gaping mouth and with long disheveled hair covering her naked body.

Kali spread her tongue over the battlefield and licked the demon's falling blood before it could touch the ground. Thus new demons could not be spawned, enabling Skanda to attack and kill Raktabija and all his duplicates with ease.

Skanda (Kartikeya) commander of celestial armies; South Indian idol

Parvati with her two sons Ganesha to her right and Kartikeya to her left; stone carving from North India

Kali with tongue spread out to drink
Raktabija's blood; South Indian
bronze

Skanda thanked his mother for her timely help. To celebrate her victory, Kali danced wildly on the battlefield, bedecking herself with a garland of heads and a girdle of hands.

Shiva Calms Kali

Intoxicated with Raktabija's blood, Kali ran amuck across three worlds, destroying everything and everyone in her sight.

To restrain her, Shiva took the form of a corpse and blocked her path. As the goddess, blinded by bloodlust, tripped on his lifeless body, she was jolted out of her frenzy. Had she killed her own husband, she wondered. She placed her foot on Shiva's chest and brought him back to life.

Shiva then took the form of a little child and began to cry, stirring maternal love in the heart of Kali. Thus forced to shed her fierce form, Kali became Gauri, the radiant mother, bestower of life.

Kali spreading her tongue; Kalighat painting

Parvati as Kali standing on her consort Shiva; calendar print

41

Parvati and Ganesha; calendar print

Parvati's Son

Gauri told Shiva that she wanted a child.

But Shiva was not interested in a family. He turned away from her and went into the forest to perform *tapa*s.

Determined to be a mother, Parvati decided to create a son for herself without the aid of her husband. She scrubbed her skin with sandalpaste, scraped off the dead skin, mixed it with clay and moulded out of it a beautiful doll into which she breathed life.

She ordered her son, thus created, to keep watch over her cave and keep out all strangers.

Ganesha beloved son and sacred doorkeeper of Shakti; contemporary illustration

Guardian of Thresholds

When Shiva returned to Kailas, Parvati's son failed to recognise his mother's consort and prevented him from entering the cave.

Irritated by the child's insolence, Shiva raised his trident and cut off his head.

When Parvati saw her son's headless body she wept and out of her tears came her fierce handmaidens, the **Yoginis**, who threatened to destroy the whole world.

To placate Parvati, Shiva resurrected the child by placing a cow-elephant's head on the severed neck. Shiva also accepted the lad as Ganesha, first of his sons.

Parvati riding her attendant
Bhairava who dances on a corpse;
Nepali painting

Parvati with her husband Shiva and two sons Kartikeya and Ganesha; Pahari painting

Shiva and Parvati unite to become one; South Indian bronze

Ganesha who had prevented Shiva from crossing the threshold of his mother's cave, became keeper of thresholds, an obstacle to all that is undesirable.

He who seeks access to the wisdom, bounty and mystery of Nature, worships Ganesha, beloved son and sacred doorkeeper of Shakti.

The Divine Homemaker

With Parvati by his side, Shiva became a family man. But he did not abandon his ways as a hermit: he continued to meditate and immerse himself in narcotic dreams. His carefree attitude, his refusal to shoulder household responsibilities sometimes angered Parvati. But then she would come to terms with his unconventional ways and make peace. The consequent marital bliss between Shakti and Shiva ensured harmony between Matter and Spirit and brought stability to the cosmos.

Parvati thus became **Ambika,** goddess of the household, of marriage, motherhood and family.

Two Faces of the Village-Goddess

Every Indian village has its own goddess known as the
grama-devi or village-goddess. She is local manifestation
of the cosmic Devi. The village is named after the
grama-devi: there is Kali of Calcutta, Mumba of
Mumbai, Chandika of Chandigarh, Syamala of Simla,
Bhavani of Bhavnagar . . .

The *grama*-devi embodies the village. Usually represented
by a head and two hands, her body is said to be the
fields, streets and houses of the village. Thus the villagers
effectively live 'in' her.

Villagers usually refer to their goddess as **Mata**, **Ambe**,
Ayi, **Amman** which means 'mother' in the local tongue.
When happy the *grama*-devi is said to be **Sitala**, the calm
one, who nourishes and protects the village. But when
angry she tranforms into **Jari-Mari**, the fiery one, and
brings disease and drought to the village.

Head of a village-goddess from
Orissa; calendar print

A *theyyam* performance in Kerala
where a dancer invokes the goddess
by dressing up like her

45

Legends of Sorrow

Legends of the village-goddess invariably reveal ancient atrocities committed against a local woman: tales of ill treatment by husband; accusations of adultery; unrequited love; divorce; denial of autonomy; death during pregnancy; Sati-burning.

To deflect the fury of the wronged woman she is transformed into a goddess by the village. Regular festivals are celebrated in her honour during which male animals — buffaloes, rams, fowls — are sacrificed to her. Men walk on fire or swing from hooks while women dance and sing. These are said to be symbolic punishments suffered by village men for crimes committed against the goddess by their ancestors.

The following are some of the innumerable narratives of the folk goddesses of India:

Bahuchara of Gujarat

Bahuchara was given in marriage to a prince who never spent time with her. Instead, he would go to the jungle every night on his white horse.

Bahuchara decided to follow her husband and find out why he never came to her. As she had no horse, she rode a jungle fowl. She discovered that her husband spent the night in the jungle behaving as a woman.

"If you are not interested in women why did you marry me?" asked Bahuchara. The prince begged her forgiveness and said his parents had forced him into marriage so that he could father children.

Bahuchara declared that she would forgive him if he and other men like him worshipped her as a goddess, dressed as a woman.

Today Bahuchara, whose temple is located in Gujarat, is worshipped by impotent men, eunuchs, homosexuals and hermaphrodites seeking redemption from a life that has cast them out of mainstream society.

Bahuchara is depicted in iconography as sitting on male roosters or fowls — thus symbolising her power over the male gender.

Ammavaru

In the beginning, nothing existed. Only Ammavaru sat on a lotus that floated on the cosmic waters. To amuse herself she laid three eggs on the lotus leaf out of which emerged three gods: Brahma, Vishnu and Shiva.

"Let us marry and create life," she told the gods.

46   Bahuchara of Gujarat; calendar print

Ammavaru: the mother of Brahma, Vishnu and Shiva

The gods refused. This made Ammavaru very angry. Her third eye located in the middle of her forehead burned with fury. In fear, the gods acceded to her request. "But first you must give us your third eye," they said.

Ammavaru afire with desire plucked her third eye and gave it to the three gods. As soon as she did that she lost all her divine powers, her skin wrinkled, her breasts withered and her hair turned grey.

Brahma, Vishnu and Shiva created the earth out of Ammavaru's body and ruled over it. From the body of the great goddess emerged many *shakti*s who became village-goddesses.

Kanyakumari of South India

Punyakshi lived in a village located on the southern tip of India. She wanted to be Shiva's bride, but the gods were opposed to her wishes because only as a virgin did she possess the power to kill demons who plagued the earth. "If he desires you, let him pay the bridal price of a sugarcane without rings, a betel leaf without veins, a mango without a seed," they said.

Kanyakumari, the maiden who waits for her groom with her wedding garland on the southern tip of India; calendar print

Shiva, in response to Punyakshi's fervent prayer, conjured up these supernatural gifts and won Punyakshi's hand in marriage.

The gods agreed to let Punyakshi marry but laid down a condition: "If he wants to marry you, he must leave his abode when the sun sets and reach your village before the sun rises."

Determined to marry Punyakshi, Shiva mounted his bull and rushed towards Punyakshi's village located on the southern tip of India. But just when the village appeared on the horizon, he heard roosters crow. Believing it was daybreak already, he turned around heartbroken. But he was mistaken — the gods had made the roosters crow in the middle of the night, hours before it was time for the sun to rise.

When Punyakshi learnt of the divine deception, her fury knew no bounds. She kicked the pots of food prepared for her wedding which turned into coloured sand found on the southern shores of India even today.

The demons offered to marry her and satisfy her longings. Outraged by their audacity, Punyakshi picked up a sickle and ripped out their hearts. She then stood on the seashore beside her village facing the sea and vowed not to move until she was reunited with her lord at the end of time. She became Kanyakumari, the divine maiden.

The cult of the virgin is popular in many parts of India. It is believed that when a woman does not enjoy the company of husband and children, her creative energy bottles up inside her and becomes destructive. This bottled energy is feared and hence worshipped.

Vaishnav-devi of Jammu; calendar print

Vaishnavi of Jammu

Trikuta wanted to marry Prince Rama of Ayodhya. But Rama said, "I already have a wife and will not take another."

So Trikuta went to the mountains to live as a hermit. But there Bhairava, a sorcerer, forced his lustful attentions on her. Disgusted by his behaviour, she left her hermitage and sought refuge in a cave. Bhairava followed her there and refused to leave her alone.

Finally, after being chased across many hills and valleys, Trikuta decided to run no more. She turned on her tormentor with a sword and after a great battle, succeeded in beheading him.

The beheaded Bhairava apologised to the goddess and accepted her as his mother. From a lustful man he was transformed into an innocent child, by the grace of Trikuta.

Thereafter, the hill-dwellers began revering her as a goddess. She came to be known as Vaishnavi, as it is said she will be Vishnu's bride when *Kali Yuga*, the dark age of spiritual blindness, comes to an end.

Meenakshi of Madurai

Meenakshi was born with three breasts and the disposition of a man. After her father died, she became queen of Madurai and set out with her armies to conquer the world.

She defeated every king who tried to stop her march. Finally she came to a hill whose resident, a lone ascetic, refused to accept her suzerainty. Meenakshi challenged him to a duel but as soon as she cast her eyes on the ascetic youth, she was overwhelmed with desire.

Meenakshi of Madurai; calendar print

As a result she lost her extra breast, her will to fight and transformed into a coy maiden. She made the ascetic — who was none other than Shiva — her consort and ruled her city with him by her side.

The cult of the domesticated mother-goddess is quite popular in South India.

Mariamman of Karnataka

Durgamma, daughter of a priest, thought that her husband was a high-caste *brahmana*.

But one day he expressed the desire to eat the tongue of a cow and Durgamma realised that he was no priest, he was a criminal outcast who, disguised as a *brahmana*, had tricked her into marrying him.

In her fury, Durgamma transformed into a goddess, picked up a sickle and cut off the head of the impostor. She became renowned as Mariamman.

The cult of the betrayed wife has taken many forms all over India and is a rather fierce cult. The betrayed wife is appeased with offerings of clothes, jewellery and flowers and the sacrifice of animals and birds.

A village-goddess in Karnataka to whom sacrifices are made when the village is afflicted with drought or epidemic

Pattini of Tamil Nadu

Kannagi's husband Kovalan was executed after being unjustly accused of stealing the anklet of the queen of Madurai. The anklet in question belonged to Kannagi, not the queen.

Striding into the royal palace she held the king and his city responsible for her widowhood. In her rage, she threw her anklet in the city square. From it rose the flames of her fury that reduced the city of Madurai to ashes.

Kannagi then went to the forest and burnt herself on her husband's funeral pyre. She became Pattini, the divine chaste wife, worthy of worship.

The cult of the chaste wife is also known as the Sati cult. This cult deifies faithful wives who preferred death to dishonour.

In the middle ages, many Rajput women committed suicide rather than submit to marauders who had killed their warrior husbands in the battlefield. Impressions of their palms — taken before the immolation — have become auspicious as, many believe, these women have risen up as guardians of female dignity.

Some misguided sections of society have used this cult to glorify the practice of burning widows which has been declared illegal by the Government of India.

Pattini, the chaste wife; Mysore painting

Hidimbi of Himachal Pradesh

Hidimbi was a demoness who along with her brother Hidimba loved eating human flesh. They lived in a jungle and preyed on unwary travellers.

One day, however, she saw a handsome stranger walking through the woods and fell in love. To save his life, she killed her own brother. In gratitude, the handsome man who was Bhima, the Pandava, married her.

Hidimbi and Bhima lived in the forest enjoying each other's company. But as time passed, Bhima grew tired of forest life. He longed for civilisation and human company.

Unable to bear his sorrow, Hidimbi let him go, not letting him know that she was with child lest he stay back out of a sense of responsibility.

Hidimbi was left all alone in the forest with her son. She became the guardian of tribals and travellers. In due course she came to be worshipped as a goddess revered by all those who venture into the wooded wilds of Himachal Pradesh.

Disembodied head of Renuka-
Yellamma; calendar print

Renuka-Yellamma of Belgaum

Renuka, wife of the high-caste sage Jamadagni, was so
chaste that she acquired the power to collect water in
unbaked clay pots. One day, however, she saw a
handsome prince sport with his wives on the banks of the
river Narmada. Adulterous thoughts entered her heart
and she lost her special powers.

When Jamadagni divined Renuka's lustful desires he
was furious; he ordered his five sons to kill their unchaste
mother. The first four sons refused. But his youngest son
Parashurama raised his axe intent on striking Renuka.

Renuka ran for her life and was given refuge in the house
of a low-caste woman called Yellamma. Parashurama

entered Yellamma's hut and raised his axe to behead Renuka. Yellamma tried to stop him, coming between mother and son. When Parashurama swung his axe, he beheaded both Renuka and Yellamma.

Pleased with his son's unquestioning obedience, Jamadagni told Parashurama to ask for a boon. "Bring my mother back to life," Parashurama begged. Jamadagni agreed to do so. He gave Parashurama a pot of holy water and told him to sprinkle this on his mother after rejoining her head and body.

Parashurama rushed to Yellamma's hut and did as he was told. But in his rush, he put his mother's head on Yellamma's body. As a result, the resurrected woman with a high-caste head but a low-caste body belonged to neither to the community of *brahmana*s nor to the community of *shudra*s. She became a goddess.

Images of the goddess' head without body, known as Renuka-Yellamma, and body without head, known as Lajja-Gauri, are found in folk-shrines all over India.

Lajja-Gauri: the headless body of the goddess; terracotta

Parashurama beheading Renuka; Mysore painting

53

Gangamma of Andhra Pradesh

Gangamma lived in the village and her presence ensured that the village was free from disease and drought. But one day, as she danced in the millet field, the villagers accused her of unchaste behaviour. Gangamma protested her innocence. "Prove it by walking on fire."

Gangamma, dressed in red robes, smeared with vermilion powder and turmeric paste, fearlessly stepped into a blazing pyre. The flames did not touch her. Instead they transformed Gangamma into a blazing goddess.

The entire villagers saw her through the smoke. Her eyes were red. Her nostrils flared as she demanded vengeance. Regretting their actions, the villagers begged her to calm down. They offered her gifts — flowers, jewels, perfumes. They sacrificed goats and buffaloes in her honour. They built a shrine to her image. Finally Gangamma calmed down.

Whenever a calamity strikes the village, the villagers say: "Gangamma is angry". But when the harvests are good and the villagers are joyful, they say: "Gangamma is happy." And so the years go by, the fate of the village and the divinity of Gangamma intimately interwined.

Such is the situation with almost every village in India that has a grama-devi.

Bhagavati of Kerala

The demon Daruka created havoc in the village, destroying crops, polluting wells, killing livestock.

The villagers prayed to the goddess Bhagavati, who rose in all her fury, trident in hand. Her laughter thundered through the dark night and shook the skies. She challenged Daruka to a battle and after a fierce fight, plunged her trident into his heart. She drank his blood and quenched her thirst.

The sight of Bhagavati's blood shot eyes frightened her consort. He ran away and sought refuge in the Northern hills.

She remained in the village as guardian, adored by the villagers despite her furious persona.

The cult of the terrifying protectress is common in Kerala and South Karnataka. Her visage is rather frightening — naked with sharp fangs, outstreched tongue, gaunt features, sword in one hand, a cut head in another, serpents all around her. This scary image is believed to frighten away malevolent forces of the universe.

Bhagavati, the killer of Daruka; calendar print

Gangamma; wooden idol from
Andhra Pradesh

55

Kumari of Nepal

The king of Nepal once invited Taleju, the guardian goddess of his kingdom to a game of dice. She arrived bedecked in gold and jasmine flowers. Overwhelmed by her beauty, the king looked upon her with eyes of desire. Enraged, the goddess ran out of Nepal, leaving its frontiers unguarded — open to attack by raiders and mauraders.

The king of Nepal, fearing for his kingdom and his crown, apologised to the goddess and begged her to return.

Finally, after much placation, Taleju appeared in the king's dream and said, "I will enter your land in the form of a mortal girl-child, not a divine woman, so that no one shall cast lustful eyes on me. As long as I am worshipped thus, your kingdom and your crown will come to no harm."

So it is that till today, the kings of Nepal worship their guardian goddess in the form of little girls called Kumaris.

The cult of the guardian goddess was popular in the middle ages. When a guardian goddess is defeated, the citadel protected by her falls into enemy hands. In the Ramayana, it is said that Lankeshvari, the guardian goddess of Lanka, was defeated by the monkey-god Hanuman and it was this event that led to the fall of the demon-king Ravana, ruler of Lanka.

Manifestations of Devi

Chapter VII

Devi manifests herself as the consort, queen, mother, sister and daughter of gods, demons and humans. The following are tales associated with the many manifestations of the mother-goddess:

Saranya — wife of the sun-god

Saranya was the daughter of Vishvakarma, the celestial artisan. She was given in marriage to the sun-god, Surya. But the glare of the sun-god hurt her eyes. So leaving her shadow behind, she ran out of her husband's house.

In the days that followed, Surya realised that the woman in his house was not his wife but her shadow. He traced the real Saranya to the house of Vishvakarma. But when he went to fetch her, she ran away from him.

"What do I do now?" asked the sun-god.

"Reduce your glare," advised his father-in-law who took a chisel and snipped off an eighth of the sun's rays. With his radiance thus reduced, Surya set out in search of his wife.

Surya found Saranya on earth; she had turned herself into a beautiful mare. Surya approached her in the form of a magnificient stallion and declared his love for her. Saranya, who could now look upon her radiant husband without squinting her eyes, accepted her husband and bore him two sons: the twin Ashwins.

Rohini — favourite of the moon-god

Chandra, the moon-god, married twenty-seven star-goddesses; who were daughters of the priest-king Daksha. But Chandra preferred only one of them, Rohini. This angered Daksha who ordered Chandra to spend one night with each of his wives.

And it came to pass that Chandra displayed his full beauty on the nights he was with Rohini. His lustre waned as he had to leave her side and waxed as he approached her, twenty seven days later. When Chandra was all alone, with no wife by his side, he did not shine at all — it was the new moon night.

Svaha — consort of the fire-god

The fire-god Agni secretly desired the seven wives of the seven celestial sages, the *sapta rishi*s. But fear of the sages kept him in check.

Saranya: consort of the sun-god; calendar print

57

The goddess Svaha divined the cause of Agni's unhappiness and satisfied his desire by approaching him seven times, each time disguised as one of the seven desired women.

Agni, blinded by passion, failed to recognise the impostor. But when the truth became known, he saluted Svaha, "Thanks to you, I have quenched my thirst without breaking the sacred laws of marriage and without incurring the wrath of the *sapta rishi*s." Agni accepted Svaha as his consort and declared that he would not accept any oblation unless her name was chanted during the offering. And so it is that during a *yagna* ceremony, the priests says, "Svaha," every time he pours milk or butter into the fire.

The child born of Agni's union with Svaha was named Agneya; he was a divine warrior with the strength of seven men.

Sachi — the divine queen

Sachi is the goddess of sovereignty. Any man who performs a thousand sacrifices wins Sachi's affection and becomes Indra, lord of heaven.

Sachi: goddess of sovereignty and consort of Indra, king of the gods; temple wall carving

As soon as another man performs a thousand sacrifices, Sachi casts away the old Indra and invites the new one to rule the heavens. Thus while different Indras rule the heavens, only one Sachi sits beside them.

An Indra who seeks to hold on to his crown constantly tries to disrupt the holy rituals conducted by rivals.

One such Indra, in a bid to hinder a pretender's sacrifice, killed the officiating priest. For this crime, he was told to leave the heavens and return only after purifying his guilt-stained heart.

Without an Indra, Amravati, city of the gods, was vulnerable to attacks by demons. So the gods looked for someone who could serve as Indra, temporarily.

They chose Nahusha, a man who had performed 999 sacrifices and hence was almost an Indra. Nahusha was invited to the heavens and crowned king.

But Sachi did not accept him as her lord. "He has not performed a thousand sacrifices," she reminded the gods.

Nahusha was allowed to ride celestial elephants, visit the divine pleasure-gardens and wield the sacred thunderbolt. He longed, however, for the pleasure of Sachi's company. He tried to win her affection with gifts and sweet words. Finally, his patience wore out and he threatened her with violence.

"Come to me on a palanquin borne by the seven cosmic sages," said the goddess. Nahusha immediately sent for the *sapta rishi*s and commanded them to carry him to Sachi's abode. The sages obeyed out of deference to his royal status.

But on the way, impatient to meet Sachi, Nahusha kicked the sages and told them to hurry. The sages, unused to such displays of impropriety, cursed Nahusha, "You fool, heaven does not befit you. Go back to earth in the form of a serpent. No more will sages carry you; you will spend the rest of your days crawling on your belly."

Thus did Sachi punish the man who did not respect her wishes.

Manasa — the serpent goddess

Manasa was the sister of Vasuki, king of serpents. She lived in the subterranean kingdom of the *naga*s known as Bhogavati and was the keeper of *nagamani*, the sacred snake jewel that counters the lethal effects of snake venom.

One day, she realised no one on earth cared to worship her. To teach mankind a lesson, she commanded the serpents of earth to bite and kill the eldest son of every household. When her orders were carried out, there was pandemonium. Parents who saw their sons being bitten to death by snakes, consulted oracles and invoked gods. All were told, "If you want to save your children from the snake-bites, you must worship the snake-goddess Manasa."

Thus instructed, mankind built temples and celebrated festivals to honour Manasa. This pleased the snake-goddess who halted the terror unleashed by her.

Those who do not worship Manasa risk snake-bites.

Jivantika — the divine midwife

Jara, a meat-eating ogress, smelt fresh human flesh in the garden of the king of Magadha. She found two halves of a newborn child.

The grim sight roused her maternal instincts. Using her magic powers, she put the right and left halves together and breathed life into the child. The child began to cry and suckle Jara's breast.

The child's cry caught the attention of the king who rushed to the garden and found his son in the arms of Jara. It so happened that the king had been given a fruit by a holy man which would make his wife pregnant. The king had two wives and he loved both of them equally. Not wanting to play favourites, he cut the fruit and gave one half to each queen. As a result, each one of them bore one lifeless half of the child. Jara had joined the two halves and restored the child to life.

Manasa: the snake-goddess; calendar print

Jivantika: the guardian of children; Madhubani painting

59

Sashti: the protector of children; bronze idol

In gratitude, the king of Magadha declared Jara as a goddess Jivantika, guardian of newborns, to be worshipped by mothers.

The cult of the divine baby-sitter has led to the worship of many fierce goddesses who personify childhood ailments like measles and mumps. Children are struck with fatal fevers if mother do not appease these goddesses. Thus the goddesses harm children when ignored and protect them when adored.

One of these goddesses is the fierce Satavai or Sashti, companion of the boy-god Sastha, whose favourite animal is the cat. Just as cats jealously protect their young from predators, the goddess Sashti protects Sastha, and all other children, from diseases. Satavai visits children in the first week of their life and writes their destiny on their forehead.

Vedavati — the hermit woman

Vedavati wanted to marry Vishnu. To win his heart, she gave up worldly life and became a hermit, immersing herself in meditation and rigorous austerities.

One day, Ravana, the *rakshasa*-king, caught site of Vedavati meditating on the riverbank. Overwhelmed by desire, he tried to possess her by force. To escape, Vedavati leapt into a fire-pit and burnt herself to death, swearing that in her next birth she would be the cause of her Ravana's death.

Vedavati was reborn as Ravana's daughter. As soon as she was born, the oracles foretold that she would kill her father. To save himself, Ravana flung the child into the sea. But as fate would have it, the girl did not die. The sea-goddess Varuni saved the child and delivered her into the arms of the earth-goddess Prithvi.

The goddess Prithvi gave Vedavati to King Janaka of Videha who named her Sita.

Sita: the devoted wife along with Rama; Pahari miniature painting

Sita — the devoted wife

Janaka, king of Videha, found Sita as he was ploughing the sacred fields of the mother-goddess.

Sita grew up to be a beautiful woman. She was also strong, capable of playing with Shiva's bow, a sacred weapon that few men could lift. Janaka decided that she should marry only a man capable of stringing this divine bow. Rama, prince of Ayodhya, rose up to this challenge and won Sita's hand in marriage.

Years later, palace intrigues forced Rama to leave his city and live like a hermit in the forest. Like a dutiful wife, Sita followed her husband into the forest, sharing his misfortune without complaint.

Sita's trial by fire; North Indian miniature painting

While in the forest, Sita was abducted by Ravana, the *rakshasa*-king and taken to his island-kingdom of Lanka. There, Ravana tried his best to make her his wife: he offered her rich gifts, cajoled her with sweet words, threatened her with violence, but Sita remained true to her husband.

The gods praised her fortitude. They helped Rama raise an army of monkeys, build a bridge to Lanka, kill Ravana and rescue Sita.

Sita — the faithful wife

When Rama and Sita returned to Ayodhya, the people said, "How can we know if Sita has been true to her husband while she was in Lanka?"

To prove her chastity, Sita walked on fire and survived the flames. But the people of Ayodhya were not convinced. They refused to accept as queen a woman who lived under another man's roof.

Rama, now king, was forced to accept the wishes of his people. He abandoned Sita.

Rama, however, refused to remarry. Never having doubted his wife's virtue, he ruled his kingdom with a golden idol of Sita by his side to represent his queen.

Meanwhile, there rose from the ruins of Lanka a demon with a thousand heads who spread terror wherever he went. When he appeared on the frontiers of Ayodhya, Rama confronted him with his mighty army but failed to subdue him.

61

"Only a chaste woman can kill this demon," said the oracles.

So the women of the city were asked to hurl weapons at the demon; but the demon stood his ground.

Terrified, the people of Ayodhya turned to Sita.

Sita, who lived alone in the forest after her rejection by the people, entered the battlefield armed with Shiva's bow. She raised her weapon and shot an arrow right through the demon's heart. He fell dead at her feet.

Now convinced of Sita's purity, the people of Ayodhya begged her to return to the city. But she refused. Instead she returned whence she had come — into the earth.

Radha — the beloved of Krishna

Radha, the milkmaid, was given in marriage to Rayana. But her heart belonged to Krishna, the divine cowherd of Gokul. On moonlit nights, beckoned by the music of his flute, she would leave her house, risk infamy, ignore danger, and go to the banks of Yamuna to be by Krishna's side. Together they would dance and sing in the flowery meadows of Madhuvana.

But alas, a time came when Krishna had to leave Madhuvana and go to Mathura to fulfil his destiny as guardian of earth. As he rode away, Krishna gave up his flute, for without Radha his music lacked the flavour of love.

It is said, Krishna conceived the cosmos inspired by Radha's beauty. Though united in heaven, Krishna and Radha were forever apart on earth, their longing transforming into man's insatiable desire to become one with the divine.

Radha and Krishna in Madhuvana; Pahari painting

Rukmini feeding Krishna at Dwarka;
contemporary painting

Rukmini — Krishna's queen

Krishna moved from Mathura to the island-kingdom of
Dwarka. His fame as the warrior who stood up against
tyranny spread far and wide and won him the admiration
of Rukmini, princess of Vidarbha.

Determined to marry Krishna, and not the man selected
by her brother, Rukmini secretly sent a letter to Krishna
requesting him to accept her as his wife. Krishna agreed
and managed to carry her off in his chariot right before
her kinsmen's eyes.

Rukmini became Krishna's chief queen and the mother
of his sons.

Once, Krishna picked up his bow and prepared to do
battle with the demon Naraka, who claimed he could be
killed by no man. Rukmini, who had always wanted to
watch Krishna fight, decided to accompany him. Together
they rode into battle.

The battle was fierce. Naraka and Krishna attacked
each other with missiles but the demon stood his ground.
Naraka finally hurled a mace at Krishna which hit
Rukmini instead. Enraged, Rukmini picked up Krishna's
mace and hurled it at Naraka. The weapon cracked the
demon's skull and killed him instantly.

And so it was that the demon who could be killed
by no man was killed by a woman, Krishna's queen,
Rukmini.

63

Revati — Balarama's wife

Revati's father Reva wanted the perfect groom for his daughter. So father and daughter went to consult Brahma, the lord of all beings. The consultation lasted a thousand years.

Reva, oblivious of the passage of time, returned to earth only to find that world had changed dramatically since his departure — humans were now of shorter stature.

Revati looked now a giant amongst humans. And men, not used to looking up to women, did not find her desirable. This made Revati very unhappy.

Meanwhile, Balarama, Krishna's elder brother, had decided only to marry a woman who could match him in strength and spirit.

Balarama, a man of bucolic disposition with a fondness for wine, was fascinated by Revati's height and strength. He discovered that she could wrestle with him and drink as much wine as he could. Much pleased, he decided to marry this strong and mighty woman.

Balarama and his consort Revati; temple wall carving

Balarama dragging the river-goddess Yamuna with his plough; Pahari painting

Yamuna — the river-goddess

Once Balarama and Revati were sporting in a grove on the banks of the river Yamuna. It was a hot day and Balarama wanted to swim in Yamuna. As he was too tired to go to the river, he requested the river to come to him.

The river-goddess Yamuna, however, refused to divert her course to please Balarama. Enraged by her attitude,

The river-goddess Ganga getting trapped on Shiva's matted locks; calendar print

Balarama caught her by the hair and dragged her through the grove. As Yamuna struggled to free herself, the river twisted and turned. And so it is that the river Yamuna has a very tortuous course.

Balarama succeeded in taming Yamuna. He established canals that helped irrigate fields. Thus Balarama became lord of agriculture and is often shown in images holding a plough.

Ganga — the river of heaven

The river goddess Ganga lived in the heavens, watering the gardens of the gods. There she was known as Mandakini. When Brahma told her to descend upon earth and cleanse mankind, she said, "If someone does not break my fall, my waters will split the mountains and wash away the earth."

Anasuya feeding the three gods as a mother; calendar print

So mankind turned to Shiva who stood atop Mount Kailasa, arms akimbo, ready to capture Ganga in his mighty locks as she descended from the heavens.

Every creature in the cosmos witnessed Ganga's spectacular descent. She dived with the force of ten thousand torrential rivers and fell right on top of Shiva's head. She found herself getting entangled in his thick hair; the matted curls and dense knots held her waters, firmly restraining her flow. Chained by Shiva's tresses, Ganga finally emerged out of Shiva's topknot, not as a gush but as a mere trickle that gently moved towards the sea, fertilising the earth on its way.

Anasuya — the chaste hostess

Anasuya, wife of sage Atri, was renowned for her chastity. To test her, the gods Shiva, Vishnu and Brahma came to her house disguised as young sages and asked her to feed them unclothed.

In keeping with the laws of hospitality, Anasuya agreed to comply with this strange request. But when she brought the food, such was the power of her chastity that the gods turned into little children, oblivious to her nakedness.

Anasuya nursed the three gods like a mother and won the admiration of all beings.

Arundhati — the model of virtue

Once Shiva entered a hermitage of the seven celestial sages. The wives of six of the sages were smitten by his beauty.

Only Arundhati, wife of the sage Vasishtha, remained unaffected by Shiva's charms. She remained true to her husband.

Pleased with her restraint, Shiva declared that she would be the Arundhati star in the sky located next to the *sapta rishi* constellation, sitting next to her husband Vasishtha.

On wedding nights, women are shown the Arundhati star that is found next to the Great Bear constellation. She has come to be the model of wifely virtue.

Lopamudra — the demanding wife

Agastya lived like a hermit in the forest. One night, in a dream, he saw his ancestors suffering because he had not fathered any children. To allay their suffering, he decided to get married.

Agastya chose Lopamudra as his wife. But Lopamudra refused to come to him until he had built a house of stone and bedecked himself with silk and gold.

Agastya had no choice but to do as he was told. He went round the world and finally collected enough wealth to build a stone house for Lopamudra and to dress up as a man worthy of her affections.

Lopamudra joined her husband and matched him in wit and intelligence, writing verses that explained the mysteries of the cosmos.

Savitri — the saviour

Savitri was a princess who fell in love with a woodcutter called Satyavan. The astrologers predicted that Satyavan would die within the year. Savitri married him nevertheless.

A year later, as foretold, the god of death Yama came to snatch away Satyavan's life. As Savitri watched helplessly, Yama hurled his noose and pulled out Satyavan's life-breath.

Savitri followed Yama as he made his way south, to the land of the dead. "Stop following me," said Yama. "Go back to the land of the living and cremate your husband's dead body."

"I would rather follow my beloved to the land of the dead," said Savitri.

Arundhati: the chaste wife; South Indian bronze

Yama tried in vain to give Savitri the slip. Finally, exasperated by her determination, he offered her a boon "Anything to get you off my back. Anything but the life of your husband."

"Let me bear a hundred sons by Satyavan," said Savitri.

"So be it," said Yama and continued on his journey. Some time later, he found Savitri still following him.

"I thought you agreed not to follow me after accepting my boon," said Yama.

"Yes, I did. But you see you promised me a hundred sons by Satyavan. How can I conceive them unless I am with my husband?"

Suddenly Yama realised that Savitri had tricked him: she had asked for a boon that could only be realised if he let Satyavan relive. He had therefore no recourse but to release Satyavan's life-breath.

Satyavan was resurrected and he gave Savitri a hundred sons. Since that day, women in India venerate Savitri, the woman whose intelligence and determination saved her husband from the jaws of death.

Savitri appealing to Yama, god of death, as her husband lies dead; Kalighat painting

68

Devi in Foreign Lands

Goddess-worship was once common all over the world. Over the centuries, however, it has been on the decline. Many scholars have attributed this to male domination of human society. Today very few religions give an almighty status to the goddess.

The following are tales of goddesses from other lands. Some are still revered, though most have long been forgotten.

Amaterasu of Japan

The emperors of Japan claim spiritual descent from Amaterasu, the sun-goddess of the Shinto religion.

Amaterasu was the daughter of the primeval couple Izanami and Izanagi. She hid in rock cave after her brother Susan-o, the storm god, defiled her sacred abode.

Amaterasu's absence made the world go dark. To woo her out, the gods came up with a plan. First, they placed a copper mirror at the entrance of the cave. Then, they got the goddess of joy, No-Uzume, to entertain them with song, dance and jokes.

As No-Uzume performed, the gods clapped and laughed. Amaterasu crept out of her cave, curious to find out what was the cause of all this hilarity. As she emerged she caught sight of her reflection on the mirror. Dazzled by her own radiance, she returned to earth and brought light and warmth back into the world.

The Sun-goddess Amaterasu of Japan

Kwan-yin of the Orient

Mahayana Buddhism spread across Central and East Asia in the early centuries of the Christian era. This religion prescribes the adoration of the compassionate and wise Bodhisattva who strives for other people's spiritual liberation.

In the Orient the Bodhisattva's grace was identified with maternal love and he came to be worshipped as a woman called Kwan-yin.

According to a Chinese narrative, Kwan-yin was persecuted by her father, the emperor, for having fallen in love with a commoner. She was locked in the towers and made to starve.

Years later, the emperor fell ill. The court physicians declared that only an ointment made out of human eyes could cure him. On learning this, Kwan-yin plucked out her eyes willingly and had them sent to her father. Her compassion overwhelmed the emperor who had her declared a goddess.

When Kwan-yin died, her presence in the gloomy land of the dead turned it into a perfumed garden and brought relief to many souls. The gods, impressed by her tenderness, offered her a place in the paradise of the Buddhas. She politely refused. She preferred to exist in spirit in the world of mortals, helping men and women cope with pain, sorrow and difficulties in their lives.

Today, in China and Japan, millions offer prayers to Kwan-yin confident that she will stretch out her hand to help all those in need.

Kwan-yin, the compassionate deliverer of all beings, who in worshipped in China

Ishtar of Mesopotamia

For two thousand years before the birth of Christ, the cult of mother-goddess Ishtar dominated Mesopotamia (modern Iraq) and the Near East (Palestine).

Known variously as Astarte, Anahita and Inanna, Ishtar was worshipped by the kings as the goddess of sovereignty, by merchants as the goddess of luck, by farmers as the goddess of fertility and by women as the goddess of beauty.

Her priests patronised emasculation and religious harlotry which earned her much notoriety. This eventually led to the downfall of her cult.

Ishtar, goddess of life, was in love with the handsome shepherd Tammuz, as was her twin sister, Ereshkigal, goddess of death. Ishtar wanted Tammuz alive so that they could enjoy the pleasures of life. Ereshkigal wanted him dead so that he could sit beside her on the throne of the netherworld.

Ereshkigal ordered her messengers to abduct Tammuz and bring him to the land of the dead. When Ishtar learnt of the abduction, she was furious. She mounted her war-chariot and rushed to the netherworld.

But in the land of the dead, Ishtar had no powers. She was imprisoned and tortured by Ereshkigal. News of Ishtar's defeat alarmed the council of gods, the Annunaki, for without Ishtar no flower would bloom and no animal would reproduce on earth.

So the Annunaki forced the two goddesses to come to an agreement: for half the year Tammuz would stay with Ishtar and for the rest of the year, he would stay with Ereshkigal.

Goddess Ishtar of Mesopotamia   71

Egyptian goddess Isis and her son Horus

When it was spring, the Babylonians believed, Ishtar was bedecking herself with flowers and perfumes to welcome her lover. In summer, they said the heat burning the ground was her passion as she lay in the arms of Tammuz. When it was time for Tammuz to leave for the netherworld, Ishtar shed tears like autumn leaves. In winter, when the land was cold and bare, it was believed that that Tammuz was with the goddess of death.

Isis of Egypt

Egypt is one of the oldest civilisations known to man. It flourished 2000 years before the time of the Buddha on the banks of the river Nile in North Africa.

Isis was the divine queen of Egypt. Her husband Osiris — lord of civilisation — was killed by the demon Seth who then cut his corpse and had the pieces cast into the Nile.

Isis waded through the waters of the river, fearing neither serpents nor crocodiles, and collected each piece of her husband's body. She put the pieces together and with her magic powers managed to enliven the corpse just long enough to make her pregnant. Osiris then crossed over to the land of the dead where he became king of the hereafter.

In Egypt meanwhile, Isis gave birth to her falcon-headed son Horus in the marshes of the Nile. She protected him from scorpions and jackals, and trained him in the art of war and in magic lore.

When Horus came of age, encouraged by his mother he rose into the sky and challenged Seth to war. After many fierce battles, Seth was defeated. Horus was declared true king of Egypt and he drove Seth into the desert.

Isis became the queen-mother of the Nile valley. Her cult spread beyond Egyptian frontiers to Rome. She came to be associated with motherhood and divine love.

Hera, Athena and Aphrodite

According to Greek mythology, Eris, goddess of discord, declared that she would give a golden apple to the most beautiful goddess on Mount Olympus. Three goddesses vied for this exalted position: Hera, the goddess of the household, Athena, the goddess of wisdom and Aphrodite, the goddess of love.

No god dared judge this celestial beauty contest for fear of incurring the wrath of the losers.

Finally, the three divine contestants descended upon earth and consulted Paris, the wise prince of Troy.

Paris declared Aphrodite the winner, not because she was the most beautiful, but because she promised him the love of Helen, the most beautiful woman in the world.

Hera and Athena who lost the contest were furious. They decided to teach Paris a lesson. When Paris eloped with Helen, wife of a Greek warlord, the two goddesses goaded the Greeks into declaring a war against the city of Troy. Every Greek man was in love with Helen and each one had sworn allegiance to Helen's husband Melenaus, king of Sparta. News of the elopment hurt Greek pride. They sailed in a thousand ships across the sea to Trojan shores where a terrible war was fought for ten years.

In the end, with the support of Hera and Athena, the Greeks managed to raze the mighty city to the ground. The Trojans were killed, their women raped, their children enslaved. Such was the price of angering the goddesses of Greece.

Three Greek goddesses

Diana, goddess of hunting, killing Achaeton

Diana of Rome

The city of Rome was the centre of a vast Mediterranean Empire for over a thousand years. Though not particularly religious, the Romans were greatly influenced by the beliefs, cutoms and rituals of the lands that they conquered.

From Asia came the idea of Magna Mater, the great goddess of the universe. Some Romans saw this Magna Mater as Minerva, the goddess of wisdom. Others called her Demeter, the corn-goddess. Still others identified her as Diana, the virgin huntress.

Diana lived with her nymphs in a secluded forest where she spent her time chasing deer and hunting bears. She and her companions avoided the company of men.

But once, a youth called Achaeton caught sight of the goddess bathing in a lake. Rather than turn away, he looked upon the goddess with eyes of desire.

Enraged, the goddess set her ferocious hunting hounds upon him. The hounds tore Achaeton to pieces. Pleas for mercy fell on deaf ears.

Since then no man entered the sacred groves of Diana unless he was dressed in women's clothes.

Frejya of Scandinavia

Golden haired Frejya was the favourite goddess of every Viking warrior. She was the goddess of corn, of gold and jewels, of love and conjugal bliss. Every god, gnome and giant sought her companionship, because wherever she went, prosperity followed.

Frejya lived in Asgard, city of the gods. The giants, who lived outside the walls of Asgard, constantly sought to abduct her. When they succeeded, winter descended upon the earth. When Frejya was rescued by Thor, champion of the gods, and restored to the gods of Asgard, spring returned.

Hine-nui-te-po of Oceania

In Oceania, on the islands of Polynesia, the native tribals believe that father-sky Range and mother-earth Papa united with each other to give birth to all creatures. Their son, Tane, forced the two apart so that the children born of the union had room to move.

Tane's daughter Hine-nui-te-po was the goddess of life and death. She delivered children through the womb and consumed them through her mouth.

Hine-nui-te-po, goddess of life and death in Oceania

Maui, the hero of the Maori people of New Zealand, believed he could conquer death if he could travel through Hine-nui-te-po's body in the reverse direction: enter the womb and come out of her mouth.

He waited for her to sleep before entering her womb. Unfortunately, she woke up, while Maui was still inside her body. Before he could emerge from her mouth, she digested him.

And so it is, man, born of a woman, continues to die.

Sedna of Arctic Circle

Sedna was an Eskimo maiden who did not want to marry. She rejected all the men of her village. But then she fell in love with a seagull and went to live with the bird on an icy island in the middle of the sea.

Sedna's father, Anguta, embarassed by her decision, decided to bring her back. He went to the seagull's island and forced her into his boat. But as the boat left the seagull's island, hundreds of sea birds rose to the sky and threatened Anguta.

In fear, Anguta pushed his daughter overboard. Sedna did not know how to swim. When she tried to save herself by clinging to the sides of the boat, her father chopped off her fingers. As the fingers fell into the sea, they turned into walruses, seals, whales and dolphins.

Sedna sank to the bottom of the icy sea and became the mother of sea-creatures.

Because of the cruel fate she suffered, Sedna is quick to anger. When anyone offends her, she shuts away all beasts, so that men cannot hunt or fish. Then shamans have to make a perilous descent under the sea, into her icy abode. They have to soothe her into releasing the sea creatures so that mankind can eat again.

Sedna, mother of sea creatures, according to Eskimos

Birth and temptation of Eve

Eve of Abrahamic Faiths

Jews, Christians and Muslims consider Abraham to be their spiritual ancestor. Abraham made a pact with God (known to many as Yahweh or Jehovah) that he and his descendents would obey God's sacred laws — his commandments — in the hope of winning back a place in Paradise.

In the beginning, so the Abrahamic religious texts say, Yahweh created man in His own image. The man was called Adam. Out of Adam's side, Yahweh created Eve, the first woman. Adam and Eve lived in a garden of eternal bliss called Paradise, content in the shadow of the Lord.

In this divine garden, also known as Eden, stood a tree — the tree of knowledge. Yahweh expressly forbade all creatures from partaking its fruit. But one day, beguiled by the serpent Satan, Eve ate the fruit, and later, coaxed Adam to do the same.

For this act of disobedience, Yahweh cast man and woman out of Paradise, condemning them to suffer the pangs of knowledge — yearning, shame, guilt, and an insatiable, inexplicable, never-ending disaffection with worldly existence.

Eve was cursed for her role in the crime with the pain of menstruation and childbearing. And because of her transgression, all women came to be deprived of power and position in human society.

Lilith: mother of demons

76

Eve is not a goddess; she is the ancestress of humankind, held responsible for all the woes of the world.

Before the creation of Eve, some scriptures state that Yahweh created another woman called Lilith. She refused to be subservient to Adam or obey the will of God. She was therefore cast out of Eden and she became the mother of demons. She is closely associated with witchcraft and Devil worship.

Mary of Christendom

Like Eve, Mary is not a goddess, yet some Christians consider her to be the Mother of God, Queen of Heaven. She conceived Jesus immaculately, without physical union, without experience of desire or lust, by the grace of God. Hence she is considered to be the purest of all creatures on God's earth, the Holy Virgin.

Jesus Christ, the son of God, brought the word and love of the Lord to man. He propagated simple morality and opposed blind ritualism.

Not everyone appreciated his efforts. Some of his opponents had him tortured and crucified. Jesus endured it all silently, taking upon himself the guilt and sin of all creatures — his tormentors included — so as to purify all humanity and herald their return to Paradise.

Mary, the mother of Jesus, has been given an exalted position in Catholic Theology. She is the Lady of Perpetual Grace who stands beside her son and hears the lamentations of all beings. She sheds tears for all. In her maternal benevolence, she offers love to each and every soul who calls out to her.

Mary with her holy child Jesus; Byzantine icon

Mary, mother of God, according to the Catholic faith

Shekinah of Gnosticism

Gnosticism was a mystical cult with roots in the Abrahamic faiths. It flourished in and around the Near East and Egypt 2000 years ago and was popular amongst Jews and early Christians.

The Gnostics believed in a feminine divine entity called Shekinah, Lady of Wisdom, who stood and shone beside Jehovah, the Almighty Father. Also known as Sophia, she interceded between man and God. Visible only to the chosen people who followed the Lord's commandments, according to Jewish texts, part of her function was to heal and comfort.

It is said, as man became more and more corrupt, Shekinah turned away from him. She still exists as an angel of mercy, willing to help man win back God's favour.

Sherawali: the goddess who
rides a tiger flanked by her two
attendants, Hanuman and Bhairava;
calendar print

Bhairava

Bhairava, the lord of terror, follows Devi as a child, his fury tamed by her maternal affection. He is her guard, ready to do battle with all those who dare look upon the goddess with eyes of lust.

Bhairava is often shown holding a head in his hand, the head symbolizing men who seek to control Nature and abuse women.

Brahma, the creator, once sprouted five heads to look upon Devi at all times. Enraged by this audacious display of passion, Bhairava plucked off Brahma's fifth head with his sharp claws.

For harming Brahma, Bhairava was tormented by madness until he found refuge in the grace of Devi.

Bhairava guards Devi's sacred precinct. As the gloomy Kala-Bhairava and the radiant Gora-Bhairava, he duplicates himself to serve as her doorkeeper. He also multiplies himself, eight times over, and sits in the eight corners of the sacred grove where the goddess sports with her handmaidens and her lord.

Hanuman

In many Devi temples, especially those in North India, there is a small shrine dedicated to *langoor-devata*, the monkey-god Hanuman, who serves as Shakti's bodyguard.

A goddess in Gujarat with her female companion; calendar print

Long ago, Hanuman had helped reunite the goddess Sita with her husband Rama by rescuing her from the clutches of the demon-king Ravana. All through, Hanuman never looked upon the goddess with eyes of desire. His chastity, strength, wisdom, devotion and selflessness, so pleased the goddess that she chose him as her eternal attendant.

It is said that Hanuman protects the border of *stri-rajya*, the kingdom of women. Once to test Hanuman's chastity, the goddess demanded that he make the women of *stri-rajya* pregnant. Hanuman was in a fix: how could he fulfil Devi's wish while remaining celibate? In despair, he began singing songs in praise of the goddess. Such was the potency of Hanuman's voice that all the women who heard him sing became pregnant. Hanuman thus succeeded in his test and won the eternal admiration of the mother-goddess.

Mahavidyas and Yoginis

The goddess is always surrounded by female divinities known as Mahavidyas and Yoginis. Traditionally there are ten Mahavidyas and anywhere between 64 to 108 Yoginis. They accompany the goddess in war and join her in sport. Sometimes sensual, sometimes sinister, they are keepers of Tantrik lore. Practitioners of the occult, overawed by the power of Devi, seek the help of Yoginis and Mahavidyas in their quest to unravel the mysteries of the cosmos.

Matrika

Matrika is a group of female divinities. They are the *shakti*s of male gods, source of their divine strength and wisdom. They accompany the goddess in her battles.

The number of Matrika varies from text to text but seven are most commonly known. They are Shivani (the *shakti* of Shiva); Brahmi (the *shakti* of Brahma); Vaishnavi (the *shakti* of Vishnu); Kaumari (the *shakti* of Kumara Kartikeya); Narasimhi (the *shakti* of Narasimha); Varahi (the *shakti* of Varaha); Indrani (the *shakti* of Indra).

Matrikas riding into battle; Pahari painting

Matrika mothers; stone carving from temple wall

Seven Mothers

Shiva was once meditating in the bottom of a lake. His divine aura made the waters potent.

Unaware of this, seven sisters bathed in the lake and became pregnant. Their husbands — the seven celestial sages — accused them of infidelity and drove them out of the house. In anger, the seven women shed the embryos from their wombs. To their surprise, the cast off embryos fused together to form a radiant male child.

The seven women wanted to harm this child — the cause of their misfortune. But when they saw his innocent smiling face, their hearts were filled with maternal love. They picked him up, nursed him and became his guardians.

While the child became Kartikeya, commander of the gods, his seven mothers became handmaidens of Chandi, Shiva's consort. Chandi declared her seven handmaidens would be worshipped as virgin-mothers.

Navadurga: the nine warrior maidens; calendar print

The cult of the seven mothers or seven sisters is found all over India. They represent the wild, untamed, fertility of Nature. Pregnant women and nursing mothers worship them all over India. When these goddesses are angry, they make women barren and strike newborns with fatal fevers. When they are appeased, they ensure health and happiness of children.

Naga

The serpent is an ancient companion of the earth-goddess. It slithers on the ground, slips into cracks and crevices, hides in holes, listening to the whispers of the soil, watching seeds turn into trees. Hence, it is said, the

81

serpent knows the secret of life and death. The serpent's ability to shed its skin is further proof of its familiarity with the lore of rejuvenation.

Early man was convinced that serpents were keepers of the secrets of life, death and immortality. All over the world the *naga* has come to symbolise occult wisdom and fertility.

The goddess is herself identified as the mystical serpent Kundalini who lies coiled within the body of every living creature. This Kundalini is potential energy, to be aroused by exciting the senses — *mandala*s or ritual diagrams excite the eye; *mantra*s or ritual chants excite the ear; *mudra*s or ritual postures excite the body. Thus aroused, the serpent rises through the spine and raises its hood in the brain, revealing to man the mysteries of the cosmos.

Ganesha

Ganesha, or Ganapati, is the first of the *ganas*.

The goddess Ambika created Ganesha by scraping the dry skin off her body. She appointed him as her doorkeeper, to keep away everyone, even her consort Shiva, who wished to intrude into her private space. Since then Ganesha has become the lord of hurdles, the celestial doorkeeper. Anyone who seeks to understand the mysteries of Nature, anyone who seeks access to its wisdom and bounty, must first appease Ganesha.

In Tantrik philosophy, Ganesha is the lord of the *Muladvara Chakra*. Unless he lets this *chakra* bloom, the sacred serpent of wisdom, Kundalini, cannot rise up the spinal cord and reveal the splendours of the cosmos to man.

A snake serving as a parasol of a goddess; bronze idol from Bengal

Lakshmi, goddess of wealth, with Saraswati, goddess of knowledge, to her right and Ganesha, remover of obstacles, to her left; calendar print

Devotees of Devi Chapter X

Rama Invokes Durga

Rama's bride, Sita, was abducted by the demon-king Ravana and taken to the island-kingdom of Lanka.

Rama, the exiled prince of Ayodhya, had no armies to help him rescue his beloved. So he prayed to the goddess Durga, patron of warriors. "Give me the strength to defeat the unrighteous Ravana," he said, offering flowers to the great goddess. For a long time the goddess did not appear. In his impatience, Rama raised his bow and decided to kill himself.

The goddess instantly appeared, stopped Rama from hurting himself and said, "Nature will support you in your quest: monkeys and bears will form an army and help you defeat Ravana. Vultures will fly up into the sky and guide you to Lanka. Fishes and seals will hold aloft the bridge that will take you to that island-kingdom. Your weapons, blessed with my power, will destroy all those who try to keep you and Sita apart."

And so it came to pass, Rama with the blessing of the goddess was able to defeat Ravana and rescue Sita.

Durga stops Rama from hurting himself and assures him victory in war; calendar print

Beheading of Mahiravana

Mahiravana, son of Ravana and king of the netherworld, was a powerful sorcerer who offered the goddess Kali human sacrifice in exchange for occult secrets. Ravana sought his help to defeat Rama.

Mahiravana abducted Rama and Lakshmana, took them to his subterranean kingdom and prepared to offer their heads to the goddess.

The goddess was not pleased with this sacrifice. She decided that the killer must be killed.

On her instructions, Rama refused to place his head on the sacrificial block saying, "I am a prince. I have never learnt to bow my head. Show me how."

Exasperated, Mahiravana bent his head on the altar. Immediately, Kali summoned Hanuman to behead Mahiravana. She drank the demon's blood and set Rama and Lakshmana free.

Yogamaya Rescues Krishna

It was foretold that Krishna would be born as the eighth son of Devaki and kill the wicked Kamsa. On learning this, Kamsa had Devaki and her husband Vasudeva put in prison. Every time she bore a child, he marched into their cell and killed the newborn, smashing its tender head against the stony floor.

The gods were anxious about the Krishna. "He must be born unharmed," they said.

"Fear not," said the goddess Yogamaya. "I will ensure his safety."

At the appointed hour, as Devaki delivered her eighth child, the goddess cast the spell of sleep across Kamsa's kingdom. She unlocked the prison door so that unnoticed, Vasudeva was able to slip out of the city and go to the village of cowherds, Gokul, across the river Yamuna.

That very night, Yashoda, wife of the cowherd-chief Nanda, had delivered a baby girl. Instructed by Yogamaya, Vasudeva exchanged the babies. Leaving Krishna in Yashoda's bed, he brought Yashoda's young daughter to Mathura.

The next day, when Kamsa strode into the prison cell, he was surprised to find Devaki nursing a girl-child. He caught the girl by her tiny feet and was about to hurl her against the floor, when she slipped out of his hand and rose to the sky to reveal her true form.

"I am Yogamaya, the goddess of delusion," she said, "I have tricked you and saved your nemesis. At the

Yogamaya, the goddess of delusion; North Indian sculpture

Brahma, Vishnu and Shiva saluting
Devi; Pahari painting

appointed hour Krishna will kill you. Until then you shall suffer the anticipation of your imminent death."

Thus did the goddess ensure Kamsa's destruction at the hands of Krishna.

Srimati's Husband

A bridal procession was making its way through the forest, when it was attacked by thugs. They killed the men, abducted the women and stole the dowry.

Srimati, the bride, hid under an overturned cart and managed to escape unharmed. But the groom was not so lucky. The thugs dragged him to a cave where they sacrificed him to their goddess, the fiersome Kali, pouring his blood over her image.

When the thugs left, Srimati entered their cave and found the decapitated corpse of her husband on the sacred altar. She burst into tears.

"I have become a widow even before I could become a wife. Only the goddess can reverse my misfortune." So saying Srimati sat before the goddess's image holding her husband's head in her hand.

Days passed. Srimati remained rooted to her seat, tears rolling down her cheeks. Moved by her plight, touched by her determination, the fierce goddess calmed down. In the form of the gentle Gauri, she appeared before Srimati and brought her husband back to life.

"I shall be the patron of your marriage and your family," said the goddess to Srimati. "Under my watchful eye, nothing shall harm you or your loved ones."

Coconuts, not Human Heads

Nandlal, a simple-minded devotee of the goddess, wanted to see her in person.

A devotee offering human heads to the goddess Kali; contemporary illustration

"The goddess likes human blood. Sacrifice a man with an unblemished body to her and she will appear before you," advised a temple priest.

Nandlal immediately set out in search of a man willing to be sacrificed to the goddess. He found none.

So he decided to sacrifice himself. He went to the temple of Katyayani, pulled out his sword and beheaded himself on the goddess' altar.

The goddess caught hold of Nandlal's head as it rolled to the ground, placed it upon his lifeless body and brought him back to life. As Nandlal saluted the goddess, she said, "I seek not the blood of man but the sacrifice of his ego. Do so symbolically by breaking a coconut."

Wrath of the Earth-goddess

Once angered by the pride of man, the earth-goddess Bhoodevi decided not to let the seeds sprout or plants grow. The resultant famine caused chaos in the three worlds.

The gods begged the goddess to have mercy. They showed her the faces of starving women and children. Unable to bear their suffering, the goddess began to weep. So great was her grief that tears rolled down her hundred thousand eyes for nine nights, causing heavy rain to fall upon the earth.

The rivers flowed again, lakes and ponds were full and life once again returned to the earth in abundance.

Goddess of Food

Once the three gods Brahma, Vishnu and Shiva said, "We create, sustain and destroy the world on our own. We do not need the help of our consorts, the goddesses."

When Devi heard this, she withdrew Saraswati, Lakshmi and Parvati into her being.

When the goddesses disappeared, knowledge, food and strength disappeared too. Brahma could not create. Vishnu could not sustain. Shiva could not destroy.

Suddenly, the gods felt hungry. They did not find food anywhere in the world. In despair, they turned to Devi who in her compassion served them food.

The three gods gave Devi the name **Annapoorna**, the goddess of food and acknowledged her greatness. Pleased with this, Devi returned to the three gods in the form of Saraswati, Lakshmi and Parvati.

Annapoorna: the goddess of food serving Shiva; calendar print

87

Attributes of Devi

Veena
Lute

Trishul
Trident

Khadaka
Scmitar

Tri-Netri
Third Eye

Kamala
Lotus

Jabakusum
Hibiscus

Paan-Supari
Betel & Nuts

Neem
Neem leaves

Yashudand
Sugarcane

Kadali
Plantain

Shree-phal
Coconut

Kalasha
Pot

Bindi
Red Dot

Nath
Nosering

Karna-Phool
Earring

Kantha-Mala
Necklace

Baju-Bandh
Armlet

Hath-Kada
Bracelet

Anguthi
Finger Ring

Katibandh
Waistband

Nupur
Anklet

Bichua
Toering

Chudamani
Tiara

Sari
Sari

Cowrie
Cowrie

Naramunda
Male Head

Mayura
Peacock

Go-Mata
Cow

Simha
Lion

Gaja
Elephant

Naag
Cobra

Hamsa
Swan

Shuka
Parrot

Ulu
Owl

Limbaka/Mirchi
Lemons & Chillies

Darpan
Mirror

Attributes of Devi

Chapter XI

Physical Characteristics

Devi is usually shown as a beautiful maiden with
shapely eyes and a tender smile. Her body is sensuous
and sinuous, simultaneously embodying the beauty
of a nymph and the warmth of a mother. She usually
has a third eye on the forehead to represent her
superconsciousness and divine insight into the nature
of the world.

Her many arms represent the totality of her power.
The world comes into being only when she divides
herself into individual elements. In each arm she bears
one aspect of her manifold energy.

Usually on the left side she holds symbols of creative
energy: pot, plants, mirrors and musical instruments.
On the right side she holds symbols of destructive
energy: weapons, fire, skulls.

Kali, the goddess without clothes;
Madhubani painting

Kali's Nakedness

As Kali, the goddess is naked. Her nakedness,
embellished with blood and bones, represents wild
Nature. Nature is not just the perfumed flower and the
sparkling brook, it is not just the sky with the rainbow
and the majestic mountain; it is also the rotting wood, the
prurient flesh, the dispassionate predator, the merciless
tornado, the heartless cyclone.

Kali's nakedness starkly defies the romantic illusions
one has about the world. Nature is raw energy. She is
impersonal. Her benevolence and malevolence are merely
matters of opinion.

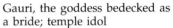

Gauri, the goddess bedecked as
a bride; temple idol

Terrified of this savage nakedness, the devotee offers the
goddess *choli-chunari*, a blouse and a veil; he gives her
jewellery, cosmetics and flowers and relates to her
through an acceptable, approachable, maternal facade.
He prefers to see only her positive side.

Clothing and Jewellery

As Saraswati, the goddess wears simple white clothes
reflecting purity and simplicity of knowledge. As
Lakshmi, she wears red, red being the colour of fertility,
the sap of life. As Gauri-Parvati, she wears green, the
colour of vegetation, of birth.

The intellectual Saraswati, who rejects materialism, rarely
wears jewels. Lakshmi, mistress of bounty, on the other
hand, is adorned with every jewel imaginable.

Goddess in her malevolent form holding serpents and swords (left) and in her benevolent form holding sugarcane and parrot (right); South Indian prints

Parvati wears, like all married women, sixteen love-charms, the *solah shringar*. These decorations acknowledge and celebrate the beauty and divinity of the human body.

1. *bindi* or red dot on the forehead

2. *mangalsutra*, sacred thread of marriage round the neck

3. turmeric paste annointing the body

4. fragrant flowers

5. perfumes

6. betel leaves chewed to make the mouth fragrant

7. black beauty spot to ward off the evil eye

8. kohl for the eyes

9. henna patterns (*mehendi*) on the hand

10. red dye (*alta*) for the feet

11. brightly coloured sari

12. jewels for the hair: tiara, hairpins

13. jewels for the head: earrings, nose-ring, necklaces

14. jewels for the trunk: cummerband

15. jewels for the arms: armlets, bracelets, bangles, finger rings

16. jewels for the feet: toe-rings and anklets

Devi with jewellery; metal mask from Himachal

90

Legend of the Sixteen Love-charms

Rati, Brahma's daughter, was a plain looking girl. No man found her attractive.

In despair, Rati called upon Lakshmi, goddess of beauty. The goddess gave her sixteen love-charms, the *solah shringar* and said, "Any woman who bedecks her body with these love-charms will enchant the man of her dreams and attract the forces of prosperity into her household."

Wearing these Rati became the beloved of Kama, Lord of love and desire. And so, women wear the *solah shringar* ensuring conjugal joy and marital bliss.

Bedecking of a bride; Rajasthani miniature painting

Sacred Mark

A red dot applied to the centre of the forehead is the sacred mark of Shakti. Red is the colour of blood, of life and fertility. The dot or *bindi* is a sacred *yantra* or charm that symbolises the root of life. In geometry, a dot is dimensionless hence the fundamental unit of all lines and curves, in effect the fundamental unit of all shapes.

When a girl gets married, she becomes a *suhagan*. She wears this sacred mark to establish her link with Shakti. As *suhagan*, she will nurture life in her womb and bring forth another generation of a family.

Musical Instruments

As Saraswati, the goddess makes music with stringed instruments like lute, *veena*. As Lakshmi, she is fond of the flute or conch that are wind instruments. As Parvati, she rattles the drum, *damaru*, a percussion instrument.

Saraswati holding lute with a peacock beside her; modern calendar print (left) and Devi bearing weapons of war; South Indian painting (right)

91

Devi bearing weapons of war; stone reliefs from North and Central India

Weapons

The goddess is the patron of warriors and is surrounded by nine fierce maidens, the Navadurgas, who bear swords, scmitars and sickles in their hands. As Durga, the unconquerable goddess, she carries many weapons. With a trident she killed the buffalo-demon Mahisha, with a sword she beheaded Chanda and Munda.

She gifts weapons to righteous warriors. The Marathas believe that in the form of Bhavani, she gave their leader Shivaji a sword that enabled him to defeat all his enemies.

Lakshmi, goddess of wealth and fortune, who provides Vishnu with the wherewithal to preserve the world; Modern calendar art

Left Side

As Lakshmi, the goddess stands beside Vishnu; as Gauri, she stands beside Shiva. She always stands to the left of her consort, left being the side of the heart, creativity and intuition, qualities associated with the mother-goddess. Hence the goddess is called *vamangi*, mistress-of-the-left-half.

The right side represents intellect, order and logic and is associated with the father-god, Devi's consort.

It is said, the wife sits on the left side of a man and the daughter or mother sits on his right side. Thus man is bound on one side by his pleasure, represented by his wife, and on the other side by his duty and responsibility, represented by his mother and daughter.

Sacred Plants

Just as women bear children, plants bear fruits hence all plants are associated with wealth, prosperity and the mother-goddess.

The goddess is often shown holding a sugarcane in her hand. The sugarcane is the shaft of the love-god Kama's bow. Another plant closely associated with Kama is the mango. Mango leaves and flowers are often used to decorate the thresholds of houses and sacred pots of the mother-goddess. The mango attracts love and joy.

According to traditional belief, the plantain or banana plant bears fruit without pollination and fertilisation, unaided by pollen or the male seed. Thus the plantain is a virgin-mother like Parvati who gave birth to Ganesha without the help of her consort, Shiva. The banana plant is therefore considered to be the symbol of goddess-power and is placed on the four corners of an altar.

The goddess either sits on a lotus or holds the lotus in her hand. For Lakshmi, the lotus symbolises the female generative organ, the fountainhead of all life. For Saraswati, it also symbolises essential purity, for the lotus is untouched by dirt even though it grows in a marsh. For Shakti, the unbloomed lotus represents maidenhood while a lotus in full bloom represents womanhood. Kali is associated with the red-coloured hibiscus or *jabakusuma* that represents a fertile womb.

Sour and pungent vegetables like lemon and chillies please the malevolent aspect of the goddess. The bitter leaves of the medicinal plant neem are also offered to the goddess who brings fever when she is angry.

Rice is the only crop that is transplanted, not sown, in the field. It is like daughters who go to the houses of their husbands and transplant joy as daughters-in-law. Hence rice is always associated with goddess-power.

*Yaa kundendutushaarhaaradhavalaa
    yaa shubhravastraavrutaa*
*Yaa veenaavardandmanditkaraa
    yaa shwetapadmaasana*
*Yaa Brahma-Achyuta-Shankaraprabhruti-
    bhirdevaih sadaa vanditaa*
*Saa maam paatu Saraswati Bhagavati
    nihsheshjaadyaa pahaa*

O Saraswati,
who is fair like the jasmine moon,
like white dew and pearls,
who wears white robes,
who holds a lute,
who sits on a white lotus,
who is adored by Brahma, Vishnu, Shiva
and other
celestial beings:
I call upon her to remove my sloth,
to enlighten and to protect me.

(*Saraswati Vandana*, sung before commencing education)

The river-goddess Ganga riding a fish and holding pots; North Indian miniature

93

The goddess of wealth Lakshmi holding a pot, seated on a lotus, with an owl next to her; calendar paint

Coconuts are associated with Lakshmi because they have great economic importance. Also, it is believed, the coconut is a substitute for human heads that were once offered to the goddess in exchange for worldly prosperity.

Sacred Animals

Male animals — billy-goats, male buffaloes, roosters — are sacrificed to the mother-goddess. She is always shown riding a male animal: as Durga she rides a lion or a tiger, as Bahuchara she rides a rooster, as Shitala she rides a jackass, as Saraswati she is associated with ganders and peacocks, as Lakshmi with an owl. Thus Devi tames the aggressiveness of the male temperament.

Killing a female animal is said to arouse the ire of Devi as a female is *janani*, life-giver. To kill a female is to kill all her progeny; it is akin to destroying life itself. Sashti, the divine midwife, worshipped in Bengal, is associated with female cats, because female cats represent universal motherhood: not only do they give birth to kittens and nurture them on their own, they also protect them from tomcats who kill kittens.

The goddess is often shown holding a parrot in her hand: Parrots are symbols of love and desire. By holding a parrot, the goddess reinforces her divine fertility.

Durga riding into battle on her tiger; North Indian miniature painting

Lakshmi: the goddess of fortune
seated on a lotus; Mysore painting

Abode

Lakshmi sits on a lotus in a marsh or swamp. A marsh, teeming with every kind of life, represents rich fertile earth and is the befitting abode of the goddess of life, fertility, bounty and beauty. As **Raj-Lakshmi** she resides in courts of kings; as **Griha-Lakshmi** she resides in homes; as **Dhana-Lakshmi**, she resides in banks, storehouses, treasuries and markets; as **Dhanya-Lakshmi**, she resides in fields. As **Shubha-Lakshmi**, goddess of auspiciousness, she resides on temple thresholds; her idol is often placed on entrances of shrines.

Saraswati, the goddess of knowledge, resides in schools and libraries, blessing scholars and students.

Parvati, the consort of Shiva, is the princess of the mountains, hence she resides on mountain tops or in dark caves.

Kali, the dark mistress of death, lives in crematoriums and battlefields, dancing amidst corpses and in the light of funeral pyres, reminding everyone that death and decay are the inevitable consequences of life.

White elephants that symbolise strength and prosperity pouring water to welcome Lakshmi who sits on a lotus; batik print

Worship of Devi

Chapter XII

The goddess is worshipped in her myriad forms to evoke her dormant energies, to domesticate her wild powers or to appease her wrath so as to ensure material prosperity. She is also seen as the means to salvation, the angel who leads man towards enlightenment and is revered accordingly.

Women performing Santoshi-ma *vrata* on Friday, calendar print

Vrata

A *vrata* is a special vow observed to ensure the prosperity and security of their household. Unlike Vedic *yagna*s and Brahmanic *puja*s, this ritual worship is open to women and does not need the intervention of male priests.

During a *vrata* women purify themselves by bathing, fasting, wearing special clothes and keeping all-night vigils. They paint ritual diagrams on walls and floor, chant special verses, sing and dance in memory of the goddess and recite tales which extol the virtue of participating in the *vrata*.

A *vrata* favours the simple joys of domestic life and rejects the austere lifestyle of world-renouncing monks. The aim of a *vrata* is not *moksha* or salvation, it is *artha* and *kama* — material power and sensual joy. Young girls pray for good husbands, married women pray for the health and happiness of the household.

The Santoshi-ma *vrata* became popular in the seventies following the release of a Hindi film. Though this 'joy-giving' goddess has no textual reference, her image has since adorned many Indian homes. On Fridays, women observing *vrata* in the name of this goddess do not eat anything sour because sour food is associated with misfortune.

Most *vrata*s are private affairs and have no fixed dates in the calendar. Some, like Teej in North India and Tiruvadira in the South, have become annual events and communal affairs.

Images

The goddess is the whole world: she is the fertile earth, the fruitful plant, the life-nourishing river . . . No image can contain her — yet in temples, images reflecting different aspects of her personality are enshrined.

Devi is worshipped as Saraswati draped in white saree holding a lute or as Lakshmi, seated on a lotus, dressed in red robes and gold jewels, bearing pots overflowing with grain and gold, or as Kali, blood-soaked, dark and ferocious, brandishing a sword, standing on top of a corpse. She is also worshipped as Durga, the many-armed warrior or as Gauri, the divine mother.

While a permanent image of metal or stone adorns temples and household shrines, during festivals a temporary image of the goddess is moulded out of clay or modeled using various plants and utensils. This temporary image is cast in a river or lake when the ceremony is over. Such a transient image of the goddess reflects the impermanent nature of life — just as the goddess comes and goes, so is life created, then destroyed.

The clay used for molding the idol of the mother-goddess is mixed with mud collected from a brothel because of an ancient belief that linked courtesans with the mother-goddess and the earth. The celestial counterparts of earthly courtesans, the *apsara*s, were churned out of the ocean of milk along with the goddess Laxmi. Like the earth, courtesans belong to none and offer pleasure to all. In ancient India, courtesans were considered symbols of worldly power and splendor as only the rich noblemen and merchants could obtain their services. As they never became widows and were surrounded by wealth and luxury, they were ritually adored during certain festivals of the mother-goddess.

Image of Devi being taken in a chariot; cloth painting from Gujarat

Purna-kumbha, the pot of bounty; calendar print

Purna-kumbha

A common representation of the goddess is a pot.
A pot is likened to a womb. It holds food and water which sustain life.

The pot is decorated with colours and sacred patterns made of dots, circles, triangles and spirals. It is filled with water or grain or sprouts — representing life.

The pot is then topped with a coconut. The coconut symbolises prosperity as every part of this palm is of economic importance. Also the coconut is used to represent the head of the goddess; her eyes and lips are sometimes painted on the coconut using turmeric, vermilion and kohl.

The coconut is often surrounded by a coronet of mango leaves. The mango is sacred to Kama, lord of love and fertility, son of Devi.

This is the *purna-kumbha*, the pot of bounty, the container of life's energies. It is also referred to as *purna-ghata* and *purna-kalasha*. It is placed atop temples, around marriage altars and on thresholds of houses during ceremonies. Its presence is believed to attract the benevolent powers of Nature and usher in prosperity.

In some parts of India, instead of a pot, a wicker basket is used to represent the mother-goddess. In place of a coconut, a metal head of the goddess is used instead.

Metal head of Gauri that is placed in a wicker basket during rituals

A woman decorating her house by drawing rangoli

Diagrams

Often the goddess is represented through abstract geometric patterns called *mandala*s or *yantra*s which symbolically represent the whole universe and hence express the power of the goddess.

*Mandala*s and *yantra*s are used in many occult practices to invoke the powers of the mother-goddess. They were once drawn during *vrata*s to represent the goddess and wiped away at the end of the ceremony. The modern *rangoli* or *kolam* or *alpana* drawn at the doorstep of Hindu homes is believed to be the remnant of ancient *mandala*s which drew into the household the benevolent powers of the mother-goddess.

Common geometrical patterns used to represent the goddess are a dot or a circle, a triangle, a square and a spiral.

Dots or *bindu*s are dimensionless and represent unmanifest unlimited potential energy.

A triangle pointing downwards represents female energy; a triangle pointing upwards represents male energy. When two such triangles intersect to form a six angled star, it represents creation. When the two triangles do not intersect and meet at a point, it represents destruction, a state when male and female energies no longer mingle with each other.

A spiral represents never-ending Time, unwinding and winding itself as the world evolves and dissolves.

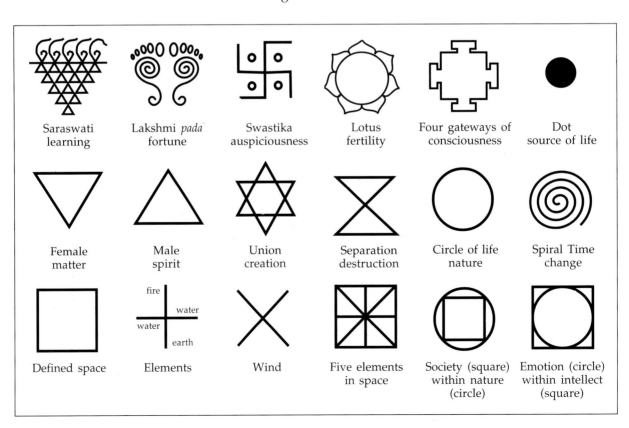

Saraswati learning	Lakshmi *pada* fortune	Swastika auspiciousness
Lotus fertility	Four gateways of consciousness	Dot source of life
Female matter	Male spirit	Union creation
Separation destruction	Circle of life nature	Spiral Time change
Defined space	Elements	Wind
Five elements in space	Society (square) within nature (circle)	Emotion (circle) within intellect (square)

A square represents infinite space, the cradle of life. Its diagonals represent the wind, its horizontal equator, water. The rising fire and the binding earth are represented by the upper and lower halves of the vertical equator.

Three parallel lines or three dots represent the three *guna*s or attributes of life: inertia, *tama*s, agitation, *raja*s, and balance, *sattva*.

Symbols

Common symbols used to represent the intangible power of Devi are the lotus, the serpent, the cow, palmprints and footprints.

The lotus represents the flowering of goddess-power. Serpents or *naga*s are the mythical keepers of fertility and guardians of secret knowledge. The cow represents the earth which is milked for food. Palmprints represent the blessings of the goddess while footprints, pointing towards the house, represents arrival of divine grace.

Other sacred symbols include the swastika, representing the benevolent rays of the sun pointing in the four cardinal directions. *Su asti* means: let good things happen.

Cowrie-shells and conch-shells are also used to depict the generative organ of mother-goddess as well as the fertilizing power of water.

Palmprints of Rajput women who burnt themselves to death on the funeral pyres of their husbands to become Sati

Blood Sacrifice

Traditionally, Shiva — the celestial ascetic — is offered uncooked food, usually milk, roots and shoots. Vishnu — the cosmic king — is offered rich vegetarian food, cooked in butter and ghee, flavoured with sweeteners.

When the goddess is Shree, the demure consort of Vishnu, she feeds her husband and eats whatever is leftover.

But when goddess is Shakti, the fiery, autonomous goddess, she is offered blood sacrifices of male beasts: fowls, rams, billy-goats, buffaloes. This practice is on the wane in many parts of India, but in ancient times it was believed the blood nourished the goddess and restored her fertility. The logic was simple: if one expected the earth to bring forth life in the form of crops, she had to be fed on life.

Cowrie-shells represent the generative organ of the goddess

There was a time when human beings were also sacrificed to please the goddess; nowadays, the ritual continues symbolically: instead of living creatures, gourds and pumpkins are cut or coconuts are broken on the altar.

101

Bridal Finery

An offering for the goddess usually includes bridal finery: red or green sarees and blouse-pieces, bangles, nose-rings, toe-rings, necklaces, flowers, collyrium, turmeric and vermilion paste. These bridal gifts are offered to please and domesticate the otherwise fierce and wild goddess.

Haldi-Kumkum

Turmeric or *haldi* and vermilion powder or *kumkum* play an important role in the worship of the goddess.

Turmeric is yellow in colour and has antiseptic properties. It keeps away germs. It is used to drive out malevolent forces.

The red colour of *kumkum* represents blood. Blood is a sacred life-ensuring fluid. So long as it runs in the body, an animal stays alive. Hence vermilion is smeared on the forehead and applied to idols and machinery to usher in benevolent forces.

Very often married Hindu women gather together and anoint each other with *haldi-kumkum* to celebrate their femininity and to wish each other prosperity and good luck. These ceremonies are ancient rituals which acknowledge the procreative powers of women through which the grace of the goddess enters the household.

Women worshipping Lakshmi; contemporary painting

Festivals of Devi

It is said that the life-bestowing power of the goddess percolates into human society through women. During festivals of Devi, women celebrate this link with the divine female: they conduct the ceremonies, dance and sing to the glory of Devi and seek to tap into the abundant power of the goddess so as to nourish their households and families.

Most Devi festivals began as *vrata*s, sacred vows and rituals undertaken by women for the prosperity of their household and the fertility of the land. Many of these *vrata*s have become communal festivals with women being sidelined in some cases as the worship of the goddess is taken over by male priests.

Women worshipping the goddess; North Indian miniature painting

Shree Panchami

The fifth day of the waxing moon in the month of *Magh* (January-February) marks the transition from winter to spring when the cold and barren earth rejuvenates herself to appear as a shy nymph bedecked with yellow mustard flowers. In North India, where this transition is most marked, this day is linked to Saraswati, the goddess of knowledge, the first manifestation of the mother-goddess. Just as the colours of spring get rid of the winter chill, Saraswati drives away ignorance with the gift of knowledge. And so, dressed in bright yellow clothes, women worship her with yellow flowers. On this day, poets and artists dedicate their creative outpourings to the mother-goddess.

Vishnu adoring Saraswati, goddess of learning, who rides a heron, symbol of concentration; North Indian miniature

Gudi: banners atop houses at the start of Vasanta *navaratri*

Vasanta *Navaratri*

The first nine nights of the waxing moon in the month of *Chaitra* (March-April) are sacred to the mother-goddess.

The first day of Vasanta *navaratri* is celebrated as *Gudi-padva* or *Ugadi* in Maharashtra, Karnataka and Andhra Pradesh. It marks the dawn of a new year. *Gudi* means banner and *padva* is the first day of the lunar month. In Maharashtra, a bridal saree and a pot, (the *gudi)*, both symbols of the mother-goddess are hoisted over a pole and raised above the house. The *gudi* is directed towards the sun in the hope it will transform the bright spring sunshine into rays of prosperity.

The last day of Vasanta *navaratri*, Rama *navami*, marks the birthday of Rama, the seventh avatar of Vishnu, who became renowned as *maryada purushottama*, the exemplar of social propriety, and as *ekam-patni-vrata*, he who was eternally faithful to one wife.

It is said, Rama decided to launch an attack on Lanka to liberate his wife Sita from the clutches of the *rakshasa*-king Ravana as soon as the rainy season came to an end. But to win the war he needed the blessings of Durga, patroness of warriors. Traditionally, the goddess was worshipped in spring. Rama could not wait that long. So he instituted the worship of Durga in autumn. With the passage of time, the autumn *navaratri* overshadowed the spring *navaratri*.

Ganga emerging from Shiva's topknot; South Indian painting

Gangaur

Gangaur is a festival celebrated over several days in the month of *Chaitra* (March-April) mainly in the Hindi speaking areas of Northern India. It commemorates the union of Shiva (Gana) and Parvati (Gauri). Women in Rajasthan carry images of the goddess in processions. The goddess is revered because she managed to domesticate the hermit-god and in doing so, she renounced her royal ways and accepted her husband's ascetic lifestyle. Kama, the god of love, is also worshipped because he sacrificed his life in bringing the god and goddess together. Near Udaipur, Rajasthan, one community celebrates this festival by allowing boys and girls of marriageable age to mingle freely in a fair and choose their life partners. This is a festival of love, marital harmony and household joy.

Ganga Dassera

At the height of summer, the world realizes the value of water. Hindus transform this realisation into a ceremony by dedicating the first ten days of the bright half of *Jyeshtha* (May-June) to the river-goddesses of India, especially Ganga who descended from the heavens for the benefit of man. On these ten days, as the temperature soars, devotees bathe in rivers and remember her sacred narrative. Every evening, priests enter the river and wave oil lamps over the waters, singing songs to her glory. The river-goddess is worthy of worship because she quenches man's thirst, cleans his body and waters his fields. She also washes away man's sins and accepts the ashes of the dead, enabling the smooth transition of the soul into the next life.

Vata Savitri

On the full moon day in the month of *Jyeshtha* (on the previous new moon day in Orissa and other parts of Eastern India), married women remember Savitri, the woman who brought her dead husband back to life by tricking the god of death Yama. It was on this day, under the banyan tree, that Satyavan died in the arms of Savitri before being restored to life. And so, this tree is worshipped with flowers, incense and sweets. The women go round the tree seven times and tie threads round it in the hope that their husbands will live as long as the banyan tree.

Teej

Teej is a North Indian festival, celebrated especially in Rajasthan, in honour of Parvati, the princess who

The image of Gauri being carried by a Rajasthani woman during Gangaur   105

Gauri, the ideal mother, bathing her son Ganesha; Pahari painting

domesticated the hermit Shiva and charmed him into becoming a householder. Though born a princess, she accepted Shiva's hermit ways. Women who seek her fortitude sing songs extolling her unquestioning acceptance of her husband's poverty. Her image is bedecked with bridal finery and carried in processions.

Hartalika

Hariti is the goddess of verdant vegetation and her presence is felt all through the month of *Bhadrapada* (August-September) in lush green fields. She is Gauri, the mother of Ganesha, remover of obstacles. She gave birth to him without the help of her consort Shiva. She moulded him with the paste of her skin. The divine mother is worshipped on the third day of the waxing moon. On the fourth day the son is worshipped. Idols of mother and son are bedecked with flowers and offered sweets and incense before being immersed five days later.

Navaratri

The **Navadurga**, nine fierce manifestations of the warrior-goddess, are worshipped over the first nine nights of the waxing moon of *Ashwin* (October-November) as she battles the buffalo-demon Mahisha. On the ninth night, as Durga, she triumphs over the demon and on the tenth day, Vijaya-*dashami* or Dassera, she celebrates her victory before returning to her abode.

In Bengal, Durga is seen as a manifestation of Parvati, Shiva's consort. On the sixth day she visits her father's house with her daughters, Lakshmi and Saraswati and her sons, Ganesha and Kartikeya. On the tenth day she returns to her husband's house. Everybody mourns her departure.

In Tamil Nadu, Andhra Pradesh and Karnataka, three of these nights are dedicated to Saraswati, the goddess of knowledge, three to Lakshmi, the goddess of wealth and three to Shakti, the goddess of power.

The goddess is worshipped either in the form of idols as in East India or in the form of the sacred pot, the *purna-kumbha*. The sacred pot is set up by women on the first night. This ceremony is known as *ghata-sthapana*. In Gujarat, women carry these sacred pots on their head, place it in the centre of the courtyard and dance round it singing *garba* or songs of the divine womb that extol the glory of the goddess.

On Dassera, people worship the tools of their trade in the hope that Devi empowers them with her grace.

Durga killing the buffalo demon Mahisha while her daughters Lakshmi and Saraswati and sons Ganesha and Kartikeya look on; modern calendar print

Devi killing the buffalo-demon
Mahisha while being adored by her
two companions: Gora Bhairava and
Kala Bhairava; Pahari painting   107

Sharad-*Poornima*

After killing the buffalo-demon on Dassera, Devi rests. She sheds her fierce form and awakens as the charming and benevolent goddess Lakshmi on Sharad-*poornima*. This is the full-moon night of autumn when the post-monsoon harvest ripens and all is well. Drums are beaten to herald the return of the goddess.

Lakshmi who rises on Sharad-*poornima* night; Tanjore painting

Karwa Chauth

What is Teej in Rajasthan is *Karwa Chauth* in the Hindi speaking areas of India. Celebrated four days after Sharad-*poornima* in the month of Kartik, it is a time when women wear their bridal finery, fast and pray for the prosperity of their households.

Women do not eat until they see the reflection of the moon in a platter of water. The moon-god represents the most romantic of husbands. The moon also symbolises Shiva, Parvati's husband, who is said to be very handsome but unconventional and unpredictable in his ways. Unlike most husbands, he is no breadwinner; he spends his time meditating or smoking narcotics, yet the goddess adores him. Women hope to possess Parvati's resilience so that they too can tolerate and come to terms with the ways of their husbands and be at peace.

A *karwa* is a small earthern pot filled with sprouts which is given by older married women to new brides on this day. It is a fertility gift, an offering of the Devi's grace, passed from woman to woman.

Parvati, the perfect wife who adjusts to her husband's ascetic lifestyle; North Indian miniature painting

Diwali

Diwali is a festival spread over 3 days. The first day, Naraka-*chaturdashi*, the fourteenth day of the waning moon in *Ashwin* (October-November), marks the defeat of the demon Naraka at the hands of Krishna and Rukmini. This is a major celebration in Southern India.

The next day, the new moon, marks the worship of blood-thirsty goddess Kali in Bengal and the worship of Lakshmi in the rest of India; while the goddess of death is appeased, the goddess of wealth is beseeched. Traders and businessmen open new account books chanting Lakshmi's name. She is worshipped as **Dhana-lakshmi**, goddess of wealth, **Dhanya-lakshmi**, goddess of food, **Vaibhav-lakshmi**, goddess of fame, and **Aishvarya-lakshm**i, goddess of success. Houses are cleaned, lamps lit, thresholds decorated with flowers, leaves, colours and sacred diagrams to usher in her grace.

1	2	3
4		5
6	8	7

1. Veera Lakshmi
2. Gaja Lakshmi
3. Santhana Lakshmi
4. Vijaya Lakshmi
5. Dhanya Lakshmi
6. Adi Lakshmi
7. Aiswarya Lakshmi
8. Dhana Lakshmi

Many manifestations of Lakshmi, the goddess of affluence and abundance; calendar print

Bali-*pratipada*, the first day of the waxing moon, marks the day when Vishnu in the form of Vamana, the dwarf, liberated Shreedevi, the goddess of sovereignty and royal splendour, from the clutches of the demon Bali. When Bali agreed to give Vamana three paces of land, Vamana turned into a giant, strode across the three worlds and won the affection of Shreedevi.

Tulsi *Vivah*

On the twelfth day of the waxing moon in the month of *Kartik* this day, not long after he wakes up from his four month slumber through the monsoon, Vishnu, the cosmic guardian, marries the Bhoodevi and reaffirms his pact to protect the earth. The fragrant Tulsi plant represents the goddess. This sacred basil is bedecked as a bride and presented to Vishnu, represented either by sugarcane or by the *shalagrama* stone. Tulsi, however, is never offered to the Durga, the unconquerable one, as it represents domesticated fertility.

Worship of Tulsi plant; Chitrakathi painting

109

Some Devi shrines in India

Temples of Devi

In India, every temple building is believed to be a manifestation of Devi, irrespective of the deity it enshrines. The inner room containing the sacred idol is said to be her womb — the *garbha griha*. To mark this, a *kalasha* or sacred pot, symbol of the Devi, is placed atop every temple dome.

Temples dedicated exclusively to Devi are of two types: one where she is Shree and stands demurely as the consort of her lord and the other where she stands independently as the all-powerful Shakti.

Consort of Male Gods

No temple of Vishnu is complete unless it also contains a shrine to his consort Lakshmi. In these temples, the goddess plays a secondary role as consort and wife. Her idol and shrine are usually smaller than those of her lord, but her presence is considered mandatory, as without her, the presiding deity of the temple lacks divine splendour.

Often, the consort of the male god is said to be local woman or princess. Only by marrying her the male god gets the right to reside in that area. In South India, one finds Vishnu married to **Padmavati** at Tiruchanur, **Indiradevi** at Koiladi, **Vanjualvalli** at Nacciyar Koil, **Cenkamalavalli** at Tereluntur.

In some temples, even though a consort, the temple of the goddess Lakshmi usually stands separate from the temple of her lord. This is seen at Pandharpur, Maharashtra, and Dwarka, Gujarat, where the shrine of **Rakhumai** (Rukmini) stands at a distance from the shrine of Panduranga (Krishna) and also at Venkatachala, Andhra Pradesh, where the temple of Tirupati stands atop the hill while the temple of his consort **Padmavati** is at the foot. The reason often given is that the goddess and her lord have moved apart after a disagreement. The separation yet close relationship between the two shrines is a sign of interdependence yet independence of the god and goddess. It is interesting to note that while temples of Rukmini, Krishna's lawfully wedded wife, are often separate from that of Krishna, images of Radha, Krishna's beloved in his adolescent years, are invariably enshrined beside Krishna in the same temple.

In Shiva temples, the image of Devi in the form of Gauri, the radiant mother, stands behind the Shiva-linga. Her two sons, Kartikeya and Ganesha, are enshrined as doorkeepers. Further, in the form of the *yoni* or base of the *linga*, she unites with her lord. The pot of water hung above the *linga* represents Ganga, Shiva's second wife.

Chapter XIV

Padmavati whose shrine is separate from that of her consort Tirupati-Balaji in Andhra Pradesh; calendar print

Although calendar prints show Panduranga and his consort Rakhumai together, their shrines at Pandharpur, Maharashtra, are separate

Thus, Devi binds Shiva and ensures he remains within the temple as a householder and does not wander away like a hermit.

Shakti-*pitha*s

While temples of male gods invariably make room for the mother-goddess, the reverse is not always true. In her sacred seats, the shakti-*pitha*s, the goddess stands independently. Sometimes, there are smaller shrines of her companions and attendants — Bhairava or Hanuman — in the courtyard.

Traditionally there are said to be 108 sacred temples in India that are exclusively dedicated to Devi. Most of these temples are located atop mountains or in caves because the goddess is believed to be the daughter of mountains, **Shailaja**.

In most temples, the goddess is represented by three aniconic stones, covered by masks of three goddesses: **Mahalakshmi**, **Mahasaraswati** and **Mahakali** who personify the bounty, wisdom and mystery of the great mother-goddess. Temples enshrining this divine triad include **Mahalakshmi** of Mumbai, **Vaishnav-devi** temple in Jammu, **Mookambika** in Kollur, Karnataka.

In some temples, as in **Chamunda** temple of Mysore and **Sapta-Shrungi** temple of Vani, Maharashtra, the goddess is represented as a warrior, with many arms, bearing

Sapta-Shrungi Devi standing autonomously at Vani, Maharashtra

Mahalakshmi temple at Mumbai enshrines the tripple goddesses: (from right) Mahasaraswati, Mahalakshmi and Mahakali

Kamakhya temple in Assam at the spot where Sati's womb is supposed to have fallen

many weapons, seated on a lion or tiger, often seen subduing the buffalo-demon who sought to control her. In these temples, she is Durga, the inaccessible one — one whose essence can never be fathomed, one whose powers can never be contained. The buffalo represents man's audacious desire to dominate Nature and control life.

Legend of the Shakti-*pitha*s

Long ago when Devi had manifested as Sati, she had killed herself because her father had insulted her husband Shiva. Her death so disturbed Shiva that he refused to part with her corpse. Holding it in his arms, he wandered across the cosmos, inconsolable without his consort.

The idol of Gauri overlooks the Shiva-*linga* of Shaiva shrines

In his sorrow, Shiva began to dance. Shiva's intense performance threatened to destroy the universe.

Vishnu, preserver of the world, decided to stop Shiva's dance by getting rid of the inspiration — Sati's corpse. He hurled his discus and cut the body of the goddess into 108 pieces.

Each piece that fell upon *Jambudvipa*, the sacred rose-apple continent of India, became a holy site, a *shakti-pitha* reverberating with the power of the goddess.

Over the years, man has forgot many of these shrines. Only a few remain in human memory. These holy sites are visited by thousands of pilgrims each year. One such

113

shrine is **Kamakhya** in Assam where the womb of the goddess is said to have fallen. Sati's tongue fell in the hills where it burst into an undying flame. The flame is enshrined in the **Jwalamukhi** temple at Himachal Pradesh. At Nainital, the temple of **Naina-devi** marks the spot where the eyes (*nayan*) of the goddess fell at Uttarakhand, Uttar Pradesh.

Parochial Shrines

Devi shrines tend to be parochial, known only to the people of the surrounding areas. Thus, not many people outside Maharashtra have heard of **Tulja Bhavani**, patron goddess of Maratha warriors. And it is only recently — in the age of television and radio — that people from beyond Jammu have come to hear of the glory of **Vaishnav-devi**.

Other local goddess temples that have gained nationwide popularity in modern times are the temple of **Chamundeshwari** on Chamunda hills of Karnataka where the goddess is shown killing the demons Chanda and Munda; the temple of **Dakshineshwari** Kali in Calcutta where the tongue of the goddess is smeared with blood; the **Mansa-devi** temple of Chandigarh; the **Meenakshi** temple of Madurai, Tamil Nadu; **Danteshwari,** goddess of Bastar tribals in Madhya Pradesh; **Karni-devi** of Rajasthan where devotees are reborn as mice, **Vindhyavasini** temple near Varanasi, Uttar Pradesh; and the **Kanyakumari** temple in Kerala on the tip of India.

Chotanikara Bhagawati of Kerala is worshipped primarily by Malayalees. **Kakatapur Mangala** is worshipped only in Orissa. Other Hindus, on learning of these goddesses, are quick to recognise her as yet another form of the great mother-goddess, not different from the goddess they themselves worship back home.

Nowadays, modern temples are being built dedicated to Durga and Kali. These lack the local-rootedness of ancient temples.

Most Devi shrines are primarily shrines of village-goddesses and hence are of importance only to resident villagers. The village-goddess, unlike the wild goddesses of forests, hills and rivers, is domesticated and maternal. With gifts of clothes, jewellery, flowers and incense, her power is invoked and her affection sought so that she brings forth her bounty for the benefit of the villagers.

Tulja Bhavani of Tuljapur (top), Chotanikara Bhagawati of Kerala (middle) and Chamunda of Mysore (bottom)

Essence of Devi

Religion exists to help man come to terms with life. Through sacred narratives, rituals and imagery, religion provides a lens through which life may be viewed. In other words, religious stories, symbols, customs and beliefs create a worldview. This worldview gives the believer meaning and purpose. It explains why things happen in life the way they do. It informs the believer of his place the world and his role in life.

The Shakta tradition offers us a perspective of life through images and narratives of the goddess. Every picture, whether it is Lakshmi sitting on a lotus or Saraswati holding a lute, has something to tell. Every story, be it the marriage of Parvati or the battles of Durga, reveals something new about life.

The lessons that come through can jolt people out of complacency and force them to confront issues, memories, desires and secrets that have long been suppressed. For the Devi embodies the world, and not everything in the world is pleasant or beautiful.

The goddess separate from her consort being invoked to protect the universe; North Indian miniature painting

Durga killing Mahisha, the buffalo-demon, symbol of man's attempt to domesticate Nature; calendar print

Durga and the Untamability of Nature

The image of Durga standing astride a lion, holding weapons in her many arms, impaling the buffalo-demon, makes a magnificent sight. The goddess looks serene even though she is performing a violent act. There is blood on the floor, but the goddess is bedecked in bridal finery, smiling benignly at her devotees.

The buffalo-demon could be viewed as the personification of man's desire to dominate the world. He is the demon of ambition, arrogance and audacity who goes about trying to tame Nature. This demon believes he can dam rivers, cut trees, burn forests and flatten mountains for his own comfort and convenience. But then Durga, the unconquerable one, shrugs. There are floods and fires. Proud kings and their vast empires are swept away in a flash and man stands humbled once more.

The image of Durga reminds us that Nature is the ultimate authority. No matter how hard man tries, he cannot triumph over Nature. Eventually, everyone has to bow before the will of Nature.

Saraswati and Lakshmi

Saraswati and Lakshmi are the two most popular goddesses in Hinduism. Saraswati enlightens, Lakshmi enchants. Saraswati represents intellectual wealth — knowledge, arts, wisdom and learning. Lakshmi represents material wealth — food, clothing, shelter, fortune and beauty.

Knowledge generates wealth; wealth, in turn, support educational institutions and artistic ventures. Thus intellectual pursuits and economic activities need each other. Man seeks both Saraswati and Lakshmi but often ends up with only the one. This is because, say the scriptures, the two goddesses have a hostile relationship.

Tales of Saraswati-Lakshmi quarrels drive home the idea that intellectual and artistic endeavours are often at odds with economic and political activities. Wisdom can invalidate the value of worldly wealth and earthly power. Worldly wealth and earthly power, in turn, can corrupt and compromise all intellectual and artistic activities.

The antagonism is also expressed in imagery. Saraswati wears a simple white sari and no adornments while Lakshmi bedecks herself with red garments, gems and gold. Saraswati's swan represents the ability of the mind to transcend the murky waters of materialism. Lakshmi's lotus represents beauty that attracts bees as well as the creation of wealth and power from the waters of life.

Saraswati and Lakshmi representing wisdom and wealth of Nature; calendar prints

Saraswati, goddess of enlightenment with Ganesha, remover of obstacles; Pahari miniature

Knowledge is acquired with great difficulty and once obtained never lost. Wealth and fortune, on the other hand can arrive unexpectedly and leave without warning. Hence it is said, Saraswati is faithful while Lakshmi is fickle. Saraswati arrives after years of study but once she comes, she never leaves. Lakshmi comes and goes as she pleases. When she arrives, life is filled with colour and joy. When she leaves, there is nothing but misery all around.

Because the two goddesses constantly quarrel, it is said that to keep the two of them together in one place is near impossible. He who succeeds in keeping Saraswati and Lakshmi together is the luckiest man on earth, for to possess both wealth and wisdom is the ultimate goal of the worldly man.

Gauri, Kali and the Cycle of Life

Parvati, the consort of Shiva, is worshipped in two forms: as Gauri holding a child and as Kali dancing amidst corpses. As Gauri, the goddess is depicted wearing a green sari, bedecked in the sixteen love-charms and sitting demurely beside her husband. As Kali, the goddess wears nothing but a garland of skull as she drinks blood and dances on the body of her spouse.

Gauri represents sex and the life-giving aspect of Nature. Kali represents violence and the life-taking aspect of Nature. Thus Parvati represents the impersonal ability of Nature to create and destroy life.

As Sati, she dies and is then reborn as Parvati, thereby informing the world that what goes around comes around. That is the way of Nature. Even Shiva, the greatest ascetic, has to endure loss and the pangs of separation.

Parvati seated on Shiva's left lap; North Indian painting

118

Gauri also represents the domesticated aspect of Nature, the fields, the farms, the villages. Kali, on the other hand, represents wild Nature — uncontrollable and almighty.

Grama-devi and Rituals of Atonement

How does one explain fatal childhood fevers or a drought or an epidemic? Some say it is the wrath of God, some say it is the work of the Devil. In Hindu villages, when a calamity strikes, villagers say that the village goddess or *Grama*-devi is angry. She is invoked and appeased. Gifts are offered and her forgiveness sought. Some men even endure torture to make her happy.

To understand this practice one must understand the Hindu belief in *karma*, the law of deeds, according to which every event is the result of actions performed in the past, either in this life or the one before. As per this law, the person experiencing a tragedy is responsible for his or her sorrow.

The goddess as warrior; stone sculpture from Karnataka

Kali with a garland of male heads; calendar print

119

The domesticated consort; bronze from Himachal Pradesh

The *grama*-devi embodies the spirit of all those whom we hurt, directly or indirectly, wilfully or inadvertently, by commission or omission, as we live our lives. The ancients knew that all humans are capable of being cruel and wicked. According to them, the sorrows of life are the result of cruelties and wickedness of past actions. Rituals that appease *grama*-devi have a cathartic effect. They ventilate feelings and help believers take responsibility for their misdeeds committed knowingly or unknowingly.

Bhagawan and Bhagawati

In Hinduism, the divine personality of godhead has two halves — the material and the spiritual. Just as woman cannot create without man, matter cannot generate life without spirit. In Hindu narratives, therefore, goddesses embody material reality while the gods personify spiritual reality. The two complement each other. The female represents manifestation; the male represents causation.

When matter unites with spirit, when gods are with goddesses the universe evolves, a new world comes into being. When they separate the universe dissolves, the waters of doom engulf the world.

Bhagawan and Bhagawati, spirit and matter, support each other. When Brahma creates, Saraswati is his knowledge; when Vishnu sustains, Lakshmi is his wealth; when Shiva destroys, Shakti is his strength.

Bhagawan and Bhagawati also oppose each other: While Brahma is beyond understanding, his consort Saraswati is the personification of intellect, wisdom and cognition; Vishnu promotes detachment but his consort Lakshmi provides all that man desires — power, prosperity and pleasure; Shiva transcends worldly life while Shakti is the force of creation and destruction that rotates the wheel of the world.

The tension and co-operation between Bhagawan and Bhagawati, between the soul and the flesh, the spirit and matter, is what gives life its vibrancy, power and momentum.

The goddess united with her consort in a single body; North Indian miniature painting

Devi and the Savagery of Existence

There are certain forms of the goddess like that of Bhairavi that rouse fear, even disgust. Hair unbound, fangs bared, blood-soaked tongue stretched out, Devi dances amongst corpses, accompanied by dogs and jackals, bedecking her body with entrails and blood. Cackling, fearsome hags surround her; a scorpion crawls up her shrivelled body. Why does the goddess often appear (for want of a better term) 'demonic'?

Bhairavi: the goddess who arouses
fear by appearing as a shrivelled
crone dancing on corpses with
scorpions on her body and weapons
in her hands; North Indian stone
sculpture

Gathering a minute particle of dust from
your lotus feet,
Brahma the creator brings forth this universe,
Vishnu as Adisesha supports it,
And Shiva, the destroyer,
crushing it into powder,
rubs the ashes all over his body

(From the *Saundarya Lahiri*, of Adi
Shankaracharya, 8th century A.D.)

Demonic? Let us re-examine this word, in light of the fact that there is no Hindu equivalent of Satan and that the word 'evil' cannot be translated in any Indian vernacular. Nothing is 'evil' in Hinduism. Everything has its place in the scheme of things. So even the demons of Hinduism — *asura, danava, daitya, rakshasa, bhuta, pisacha, vetala* — play a vital role in the cosmos. A Hindu world without them is inconceivable.

When we use the word 'demonic', we are actually saying that some manifestations of the goddess are unpalatable to our taste. We find them undesirable, inappropriate, unwholesome. We would rather not look at them. But no matter how hard we try, our world is filled with images that we cannot look at or come to terms with — hyenas killing pregnant deer, goats chewing on flowers, tornadoes wiping out entire villages, fatal diseases striking babies. All this is a part of Nature. And Nature is a manifestation of Devi. Hence, the goddess is at the same time beautiful and ugly, alluring and repulsive.

Imagine a rotting corpse. The sight is ghastly. But for the maggot breeding within the corpse, that 'ghastly' object would be 'home'. What is horrible from our point of view is wonderful from the maggot's point of view. Thus, the world is beautiful and ugly, depending on where we view it from. When a scorpion stings, it stings not because it is 'bad' or 'wicked' or 'evil'. It stings because that is its personality. The goddess does not consider the scorpion any better or worse than the cow who gives milk. Just different. To drive home this point, both the scorpion and the cow are linked to goddess worship.

In goddess worship, the unsavory aspects of life and Nature are not repressed. They are expressed in art. Hence Devi is depicted as both alluring and horrifying. She is Lakshmi, the goddess of fortune as well as Alakshmi, the goddess of misfortune. She is the radiant Gauri and the sullen Kali. As the goddess transforms herself, the devotee comes to term with the many aspects of the world and learns to be less judgmental.

The ability to accept and appreciate every manifestation of Devi is sign of enlightenment. Hence, to Devi does everyone offers the salute

Yaa devi sarvabhuuteshhu maatrirupena sansthitah
Yaa devi sarvabhuuteshhu shaktirupena sansthitah
Yaa devi sarvabhuuteshhu shaantirupena sansthitah
Namastasyaih namastasyaih namastasyaih namo namah.

"O goddess of the universe, visualizing you the embodiment of motherhood, power and peace, I salute you, salute you, salute you."

122

Devi in her destructive manifestation
bearing weapons of war and
placing her foot on a male head and
wearing a garland of sour lemons;
calendar print

123

108 Names of Devi

Devotees have tried to express the divinity of the goddess through 1008 names. These names refer exclusively to mother-goddess or to her three main manifestations: Lakshmi, Saraswati and Kali. These names are chanted to invoke the power of Devi. Following are 108 of the 1008 sacred names of the goddess:

Aditi: infinity; **Ambika**: the mother; **Ammavaru**: revered mother; **Annapoorna**: giver of food; **Aparijita**: unconquerable; **Aparna**: she who wears or eats not even a leaf; **Aranyani**: forest goddess; **Bagalamukhi**: crane-headed; **Bhadrakali**: auspicious one; **Bhagawati**: supreme goddess; **Bhairavi**: terror inspiring; **Bhavani**: substance of existence; **Bhoo**: earth-mother; **Bhoovaneshwari**: mistress of the universe; **Bhumarupa**: she whose form is all existing things; **Bhutanayaki**: mistress of ghosts; **Chamunda**: killer of Chanda and Munda; **Chanchala**: fickle goddess; **Chandi**: angry one; **Chinnamastika**: headless one; **Chinta**: goddess of contemplation; **Dasa-bhuja**: having ten arms; **Devi**: goddess; **Dharini**: bearer of life; **Dhatri**: nurse; **Durga**: the inaccessible one; **Ekanamsha**: undivided one; **Ganga**: swift mover, river with cleansing waters; **Gauri**: radiant mother; **Gayatri**: goddess of verses, cow-goddess; **Girija**: mountain princess; **Haimavati**: daughter of the Himalayas; **Harasiddhi**: the supreme knowledge; **Ida**: the offering, the creation; **Jagadamba**: universal mother; **Jagad-dhatri**: the world sustainer; **Janani**: bestower of life; **Kali**: dark killer, time; **Kalyani**: bestower of good fortune; **Kamakshi**: amorous eyed; **Kamala**: she who sits on a lotus; **Kameshwari**: love goddess; **Kantaravasini**: forest goddess; **Kanyakumari**: the virgin goddess; **Katyayani**: protectress; **Kotari**: naked one; **Kshetrasvarupa**: she who personifies the cosmic field; **Kumari**: unattached to any man; **Kundalini**: dormant uncoiled energy; **Lajja**: modest one; **Lakshmi**: bestower of prosperity; **Lalita**: charming; **Matrika**: mother; **Madhavi**: earth-mother; **Mahadevi**: great goddess; **Mahamaya**: great delusion; **Maharajini**: great queen; **Mahasuri**: the great hope; **Mahavidya**: great goddess of wisdom; **Maheshvari**: supreme goddess; **Mahi**: earth-mother; **Mahishasuramardini**: killer of the buffalo-demon; **Manasa**: goddess of snakes; **Mangala**: auspicious one; **Mari-amma**: goddess of fever and pestilence; **Matangi**: intoxicated-as-a-roused-elephant; **Minakshi**: fish-eyed; **Muktakeshi**: with-dishevelled-hair; **Nidra**: divine sleep; **Nitya**: eternal; **Parameshwari**: ultimate goddess; **Paraprakriti**: supreme nature; **Parvati**: princess of the mountains; **Pinga**: tawny; **Prithvi**: earth-goddess; **Prakriti**: excellent creation; **Pratibha**: radiance, lustre, aura; **Rajasi**: roused; **Rakta-danti**: bloody-toothed;

Rati: mistress of erotic arts; **Ratri**: goddess of night; **Renuka**: soil goddess; **Sanatani**: ancient and eternal one; **Sandhya**: twilight goddess; **Santoshi**: bestower of contentment; **Saraswati**: goddess of wisdom; **Sarvamayi**: everyone's mother; **Sati**: virtuous; **Shakambari**: goddess of vegetation; **Shakti**: strength, power, energy; **Shree**: bestower of goodness; **Sindhu**: river-goddess; **Simha-vahini**: lion rider; **Sita**: the furrow; **Sitala**: the calm one; **Shyama**: dark-skinned; **Svaha**: joyful offering; **Tara**: compassionate mother; **Tripura-sundari**: most beautiful person in three worlds; **Uma**: mother; **Ushas**: dawn goddess; **Vagdevi**: goddess of speech; **Vajrayoni**: goddess with womb of thunder; **Vijaya**: victorious; **Vindhyavasini**: dweller of the Vindhyas; **Vishvagarbha**: she whose womb contains the cosmos; **Yellamma**: everybody's mother; **Yogini**: keeper of occult secrets.

The many manifestations and corresponding abstract representations of Devi (upper row) and corresponding male deities (lower row); Madhubani painting

Select Bibliography

Indian Mythology: Veronica Irons

Hindu Mythology: W. J. Wilkins

Hindu Myths: Wendy O'Flaherty

Metamorphosis of Indian Gods: Marta Jakimowicz-Shah

Wonder that was India: A. L. Basham

Vaishnavism, Shaivism and Other Minor Religions:
R. G. Bhandarkar

Myth and Reality: D. D. Kosambi

Earth Mother: Pupul Jayakar

The Myth of the Goddess: Anne Baring and Jules Cashford

Goddess Lakshmi — origin and development:
Dr. Upendra Nath Dhal

History of Tantrik Religion: N. N. Bhattacharya

Aghora — at the left hand of god: Robert E. Svaboda

Devi: Goddesses of India — J. S. Hawley & D. M. Wulff (eds.)

Note: Tales of the goddess retold in this book have been taken mainly from *Devi Bhagvatam* with inputs from *Ramayana, Mahabharata, Lakshmi Tantra, Lakshmi Purana, Yogini Tantra, Brihaddharma Purana, Kalika Purana, Shiva Purana, Vishnu Purana, Bhagavata Purana, Padma Purana* and *Skanda Purana*. Some plots, like the story of Shatarupa and the tale of Saraswati and the *gandharva*s have been taken from the *Veda*s and the *Brahmana*s. Many tales, especially those of village-goddesses, exist only in oral tradition and have no textual references.

* * *

Other Books in the Introduction Series

HINDUISM — An Introduction
Shakunthala Jagannathan

GANESHA — The Auspicious . . . The Beginning
Shakunthala Jagannathan, Nanditha Krishna

BALAJI VENKATESHWARA — An Introduction
Nanditha Krishna

SHIVA — An Introduction
Devdutt Pattanaik

VISHNU — An Introduction
Devdutt Pattanaik

HANUMAN — An Introduction
Devdutt Pattanaik